MW00814498

THEMATIC UNIT
Kites

Written By Carole Davis, Andrea Dick, and Brenda Sampson, M.A.

Teacher Created Materials, Inc.
6421 Industry Way
Westminster, CA 92683
www.teachercreated.com
©2000 Teacher Created Materials, Inc.
Made in U.S.A.
ISBN-1-57690-367-2

Illustrated by
Andrea Dick

Edited by
Janet A. Hale, M.S. Ed.

Cover Art by
Denice Adorno
Cheri Macoubrie Wilson

Table of Contents

Introduction

Kites is a fun-filled 80-page thematic unit designed to immerse children in writing, poetry, language arts, science, math, social studies, music, art, and life skills. The literature and activities used in this unit have been selected to help children gain a better understanding and insight into the world of kites. In addition, children will experience working cooperatively, being considerate of others, and taking into consideration another's point of view. A variety of teaching strategies such as cooperative learning, hands-on experiences, and child-centered assessment are integrated throughout the unit.

This thematic unit includes the following:

❏ literature selections—summaries of two children's books with related lessons (complete with reproducible pages) that cross the curriculum

❏ poetry—suggested selections and lessons enabling children to write and publish their own work

❏ planning guides—suggestions for sequencing lessons each day of the unit

❏ bulletin boards—suggestions and plans for child-created and/or interactive bulletin boards

❏ curriculum connections—activities in language arts, math, science, social studies, art, music, and life skills

❏ culminating activities—that require children to synthesize their learning and produce a product or engage in an activity that can be shared with others

❏ a bibliography—suggestions for additional literature and nonfiction books on the theme

❏ resources—Web sites, organizations, videos, and magazines to help extend the learning possibilities

---

To keep this valuable resource intact so that it can be used year after year, you may wish to punch holes in the pages and store them in a three-ring binder.

Introduction *(cont.)*

Why a Balanced Approach?

The strength of a balanced language approach is that it involves children in using all modes of communication—reading, writing, listening, illustrating, and doing. Communication skills are interconnected and integrated into lessons that emphasize the whole of language. Implicit in this approach is our knowledge that every whole—including individual words—is composed of parts and directed study of those parts can help a child master the whole. Experience and research tell us that regular attention to phonics, other word attack skills, spelling, etc., develops reading mastery, thereby fulfilling the unity of the whole language experience. The child is thus led to read, write, spell, speak, and listen confidently in response to a literature experience introduced by the teacher. In these ways, language skills grow rapidly, stimulated by direct practice, involvement, and interest in the topic at hand.

Why Thematic Planning?

One very useful tool for implementing a balanced language program is thematic planning. By choosing a theme with correlating literature selections for a unit of study, a teacher can plan activities throughout the day that lead to a cohesive, in-depth study of the topic. Children will be practicing and applying their skills in meaningful contexts. Consequently, they will learn and retain more. Both teachers and children will also be freed from a day that is broken into unrelated segments of isolated drill and practice.

Why Cooperative Learning?

Besides academic skills and content, children need to learn social skills. No longer can this area of development be taken for granted. Children must learn to work cooperatively in groups in order to function well in modern society. Group activities should be a regular part of school life, and teachers should consciously include social objectives as well as academic objectives in their planning. For example, a group working together to write a report may need to select a leader. The teacher should make this clear to the children and monitor the qualities of good leader-follower group interactions just as he or she would state and monitor the academic goals of the project.

Why Big Books?

An excellent cooperative, whole language activity is the production of big books. Groups of children or the whole class can apply their language skills, content knowledge, and creativity to produce a big book that becomes a part of the classroom library to be read and reread. These books make excellent culminating projects for sharing beyond the classroom with parents, librarians, other classes, etc.

Why Journals?

Each day your children should have the opportunity to write in a journal. They may respond to a book or an event in history, write about a personal experience, or answer a general "question of the day" posed by the teacher. Cumulative journals provide an excellent means of documenting children's writing progress.

The Great Kite Book

By Norman Schmidt

Summary

Kites are found all around the world. They have many purposes and come in a variety of shapes and sizes. Kites can be simple or very complex. The Great Kite Book provides an easy-to-understand explanation of the parts of a kite, how to make simple kites, how to launch a kite, and the safety rules needed to be a successful kite flier.

The outline below is a suggested plan for using various activities that are presented in this unit. You can adapt these ideas to fit your own classroom situation.

Sample Plan

Lesson 1

- Begin KWL Chart (page 8).
- Assemble Kites Minibook, one per child (pages 9–12); read together.
- Observe, write about, and illustrate kites the children have seen (page 6, Enjoying the Book, #1).
- Read *The Great Kite Book*.
- Make kite cookies (pages 64 and 65).
- Begin SSR (page 7, #1).
- Assign Homework Task Card 1 (page 73).

Lesson 2

- Begin the process of recording Wind Movement (page 7, #2).
- Reread *The Great Kite Book*.
- Label and decorate a variety of kites (pages 14–17).
- Make Pinwheel Kites (page 61).
- Add learned facts to KWL Chart (page 8).
- Explore information about Kites Around the World (pages 57 and 58).
- Create a kite map (page 42).
- Assign Homework Task Card 2 (page 73).

Lesson 3

- Discuss Kite Safety (page 49).
- Make Kite Safety Minibooks (pages 50–53).
- Create kite journals (page 7, #3).
- Complete the kite crossword puzzles (pages 18 and 19).
- Learn some Amazing Kite Facts (page 60).
- Continue wind measurements (page 48).
- Add learned facts to KWL Chart (page 8).
- Continue SSR.
- Assign Homework Task Card 3 (page 73).

Lesson 4

- Continue wind measurements (page 48).
- Write kites acrostics (page 7, #10).
- Conduct a Read-Write-Listen lesson (page 38).
- Try to Break the Code! (page 56).
- Continue SSR.
- Assign Homework Task Card 4 (page 73).

Lesson 5

- Make conclusions based on the gathered wind measurements (page 48).
- Try I Spy! (page 55).
- Teach some Kite Songs (page 40).
- Complete the Kite Word Search (page 46).

Overview of Activities

Setting the Stage

1. Prepare the classroom for the *Kites* unit. Locate kite books and materials (Bibliography, pages 76 and 77; Resources, page 78). Use your school or community library to locate additional materials. If possible, you may also want to visit some kite Web sites (page 66).

2. Hang real kites by suspending them from the ceiling or tacking them on your classroom walls. This will add a great visual display to refer to throughout the unit.

3. Create The Kite Stuff bulletin board (page 69). Using construction paper or tagboard, allow each child to color and cut out the Kite Cover Pattern (page 22). Add ribbon or yarn tails to the bottom of the kites. Have each child write his or her name on the front of the kite; display on the prepared bulletin board.

4. Prepare a KWL chart (page 8). Use the generated child-centered facts and questions to plan activities for the unit.

5. Using two basic kite types—Flat and Box—set up a comparison and contrast chart (see the example on the bottom of page 41).

6. Create and display a kite-safety chart using simple sentences. If desired, draw diagrams to accompany each safety rule (page 49).

7. Learn to sing some of the Kite Songs (page 40). Develop movement activities to accompany the music.

8. Set up a word-bank bulletin board (page 20) and have the children work together to build kite poems. Display created poems on reproduced kite writing patterns (pages 23 and 24).

Enjoying the Book

1. Introduce *The Great Kite Book* by asking the children to name places where they have seen kites. Possibilities include parks, beaches, playgrounds, and fields. Ask if they can describe the shapes and designs of the kites they have seen. Have the children illustrate these kites. For homework, have the children ask family members what types of kites the family has flown.

2. Read the introduction of *The Great Kite Book*. Discuss the basic parts of a kite using the kite diagram sheets (pages 14–17; answer key, page 79); display the labeled kite sheets.

3. Reproduce and laminate the kite sheets (pages 14–17) to create write-on-wipe-off practice mats. Using erasable markers and an eraser, encourage the children to label the kites as a free-time or planned center experience.

4. Discuss kite-safety issues (page 49).

Overview of Activities *(cont.)*

Extending the Book

1. Provide the children with a selection of fiction and nonfiction kite books for daily SSR (Sustained Silent Reading). Encourage them to tell you new facts or information they discover. Add these facts to the learned section of your KWL chart (page 8).

2. Discuss wind speed using the Beaufort wind scale (page 48). Set up two or three observation posts at various locations around the school. Check the posts at two regular times each day and record the results.

3. Create kite journals (page 21). To create covers, copy the pattern (page 22) onto construction paper or tagboard. Using the pattern of your choice (pages 23 and 24) as writing pages, reproduce and staple the desired number of pages to the cover at the top of the kite. Using ribbon or yarn, add a tail to the bottom of each kite cover. Use the kite books as daily writing journals or to record and illustrate facts from the Learned section of the KWL Chart (page 8).

4. Find photographs or illustrations of kites from around the world (pages 57 and 58). Discover how kites are, or have been, used in various countries (page 59).

5. Take a walk around the school or the neighborhood and map out safe kiting areas.

6. Study weather conditions for the best kite-flying weather.

7. Begin collecting the materials needed for creating a Sled kite. Page 68 describes the steps for making this type of kite.

8. Have the children use computer software programs to write and illustrate created kite stories (see Story Mapping, page 35).

9. If possible, set up mail pals to share stories and experiences with other children from all over the world. An alternative could be to visit some of the kite Web sites listed on page 66.

10. Make an acrostic display using the word KITES. Working in small, cooperative groups, have each group create and illustrate an acrostic card chart.

    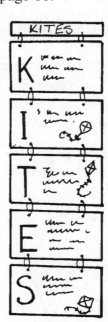

    - Provide each group with six 5" x 7" (13 cm x 18 cm) index cards.

    - Each group writes one letter from the word "kites" on the far left of each card. The remaining card will be the title card. Have the children write the full word KITES on it.

    - The children then write a sentence about kites that begin with the letter on each card.

    - The children complete the project by illustrating each sentence.

KWL Chart

The KWL Chart is a graphic organizer that helps children categorize their thoughts. The chart has three sections: prior knowledge (Know), curiosity knowledge (Want to Know), and acquired knowledge (Learned). For maximum benefit, prepare the chart in advance by listing the three labeled sections on a large piece of butcher or flip-chart paper. Display the chart so all can see. Have the children tell you what they know about kites. List their shared prior knowledge in the first section. Ask children to tell you what they want to know about kites. List their responses in the second section. Begin teaching information about kites.

The last section is periodically filled in as facts are learned about kites. When a Learned fact is discovered that answers a question listed in the Want to Know section indicate this by placing a colored dot beside the question in the second section and writing the learned knowledge in the third section, using a corresponding color marker.

Know	Want to Know	Learned
Kites fly. Kites have different shapes. Kites need wind to fly.	How do kites fly? How does wind speed affect kite flying? Where can you fly kites?	(Completed as facts are discovered.)

KWL charts serve as an excellent, child-centered resource for providing authentic assessment for teachers. They can also be a source of information for your children as they write stories, illustrate child-created books, and review unit facts.

A High-Flying Idea: Enlarge the kite pattern (page 22). Reproduce and cut out three kites. Label each kite as you would for each section of a standard KWL chart; fill in as directed above.

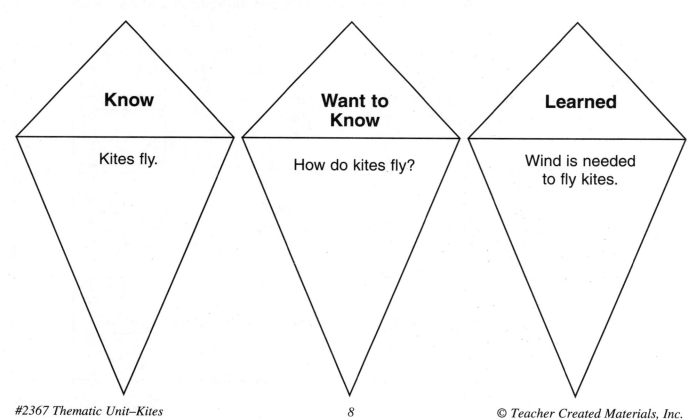

Kites Minibook

I Love Kites!

My name is _____. I love kites!

1

There are many different kinds of kites. Some kites need tails to fly.

2

Kites Minibook *(cont.)*

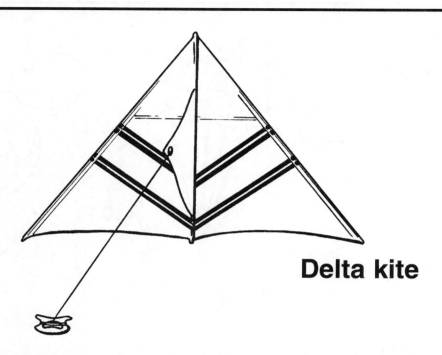

Delta kite

Some kites are flat. Some are shaped like a triangle.

3

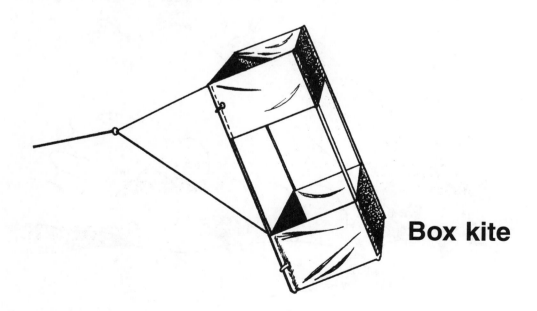

Box kite

Box kites are not flat. Some kites are three-dimensional.

4

Kites Minibook *(cont.)*

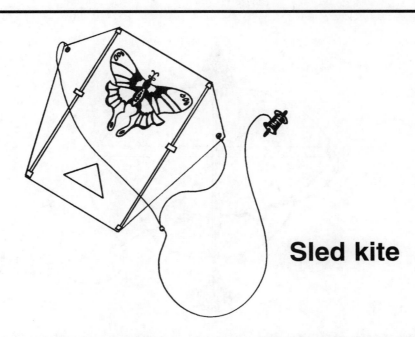

Sled kite

The Sled kite looks like a sled. It is easy to fly because it bends in the wind.

5

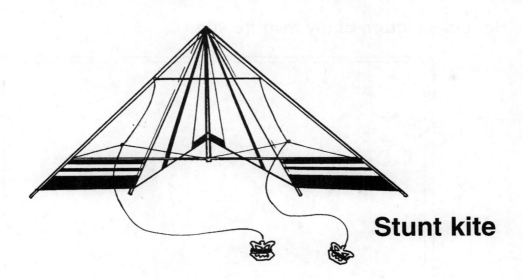

Stunt kite

Stunt kites have two or four flying lines. You need two hands to fly them. Stunt kites move very fast and can do many tricks.

6

Kites Minibook *(cont.)*

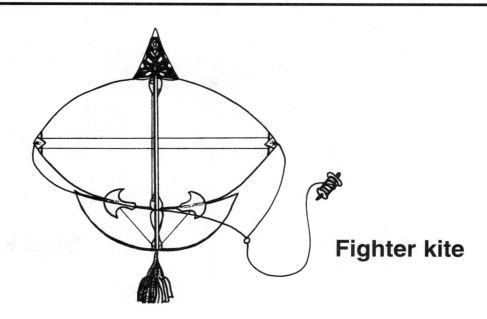

Fighter kite

Some kites are made to play games. Kite games are played in India and Asia.

7

Here is a picture of my favorite kite.

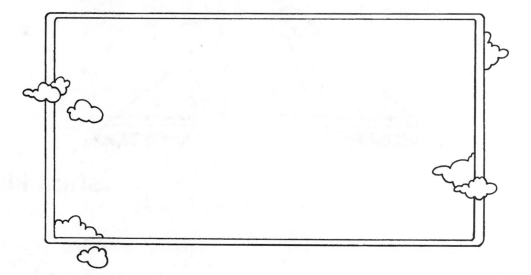

My favorite kite is a _____ **kite.**

8

Types of Kites

Reread *The Great Kite Book*, focusing on these four types of kites: Flat, Delta, Sled, and Stunt. (**Note:** See page 79 for the labeled parts of each type of kite.) Place the children in small groups and have them research these types of kites using available resources (Bibliography, pages 76 and 77; Resources, page 78). Using large poster or flip-chart paper, have each group draw, color, decorate, and label one type of kite. Have each group share their findings.

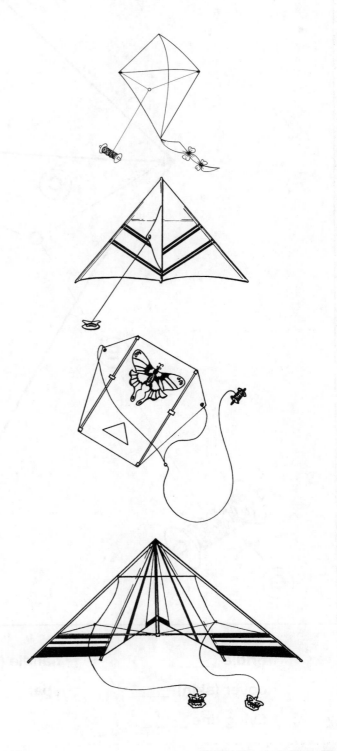

Flat Kite

Most early, historical kites were Flat kites. They are two-dimensional, do not bend in the wind, and require one or more tails and vents for stability. Many traditional Asian and Greek kites are examples of Flat kites.

Delta Kite

A Delta kite is good for novice kite fliers because it can adjust and bend to the changes of the wind. It is triangular in shape and is named for the fourth letter in the Greek alphabet.

Sled Kite

Invented by William Allison, the Sled kite got its name from the fact that Allison thought it looked like a snow sled in the sky. It is a great kite for beginning fliers because it is easy to make and almost never fails to fly. If the dimensions are correct—it's guaranteed to fly!

Stunt Kite

A Stunt kite has two or four flying lines and is able to perform aerobatics. Stunt kites come in a variety of designs and are usually made of rip-stop nylon or plastic. They also have graphite or fiberglass spars (supporting rods) to help keep them light weight, yet strong.

The Flat Kite

Match the different parts of a kite with the diagram below by writing the letters on the lines at the bottom of the page.

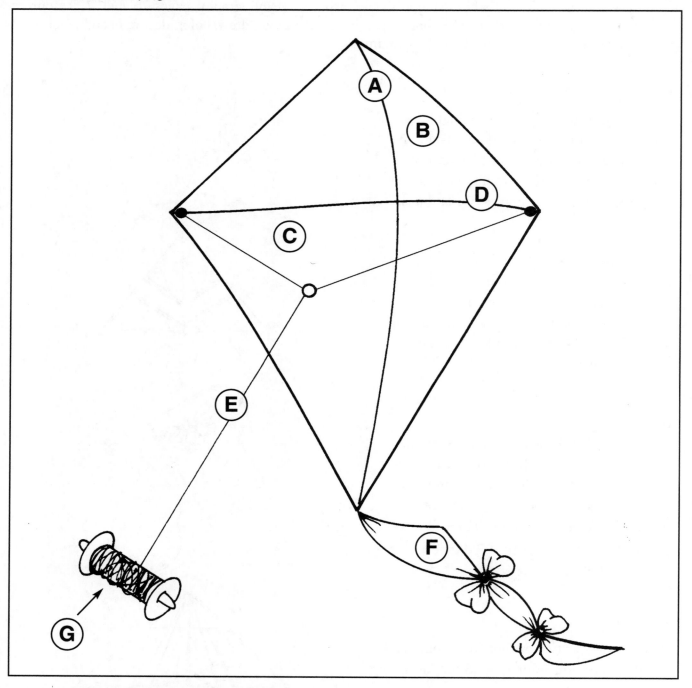

bridle _____   handle (spool) _____   spine _____

cover (skin) _____   spar _____   tail _____

flying line _____

The Delta Kite

Match the different parts of a kite with the diagram below by writing the letters on the lines at the bottom of the page.

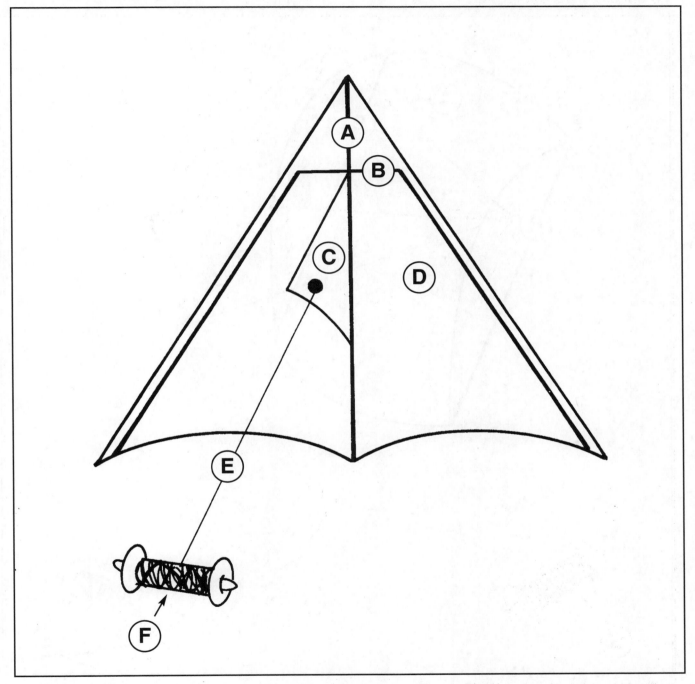

cover (skin) _____   **handle (spool)** _____   **spars** _____

flying line _____   **keel** _____   **spine** _____

The Sled Kite

Match the different parts of a kite with the diagram below by writing the letters on the lines at the bottom of the page.

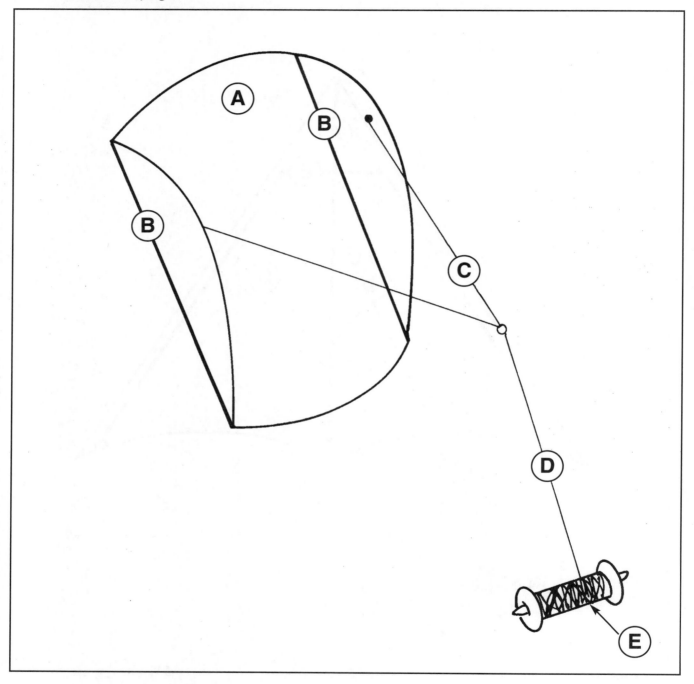

bridle _____   **flying line** _____   **spines** _____

cover (skin) _____   **handle (spool)** _____

The Stunt Kite

Match the different parts of a kite with the diagram below by writing the letters on the lines at the bottom of the page.

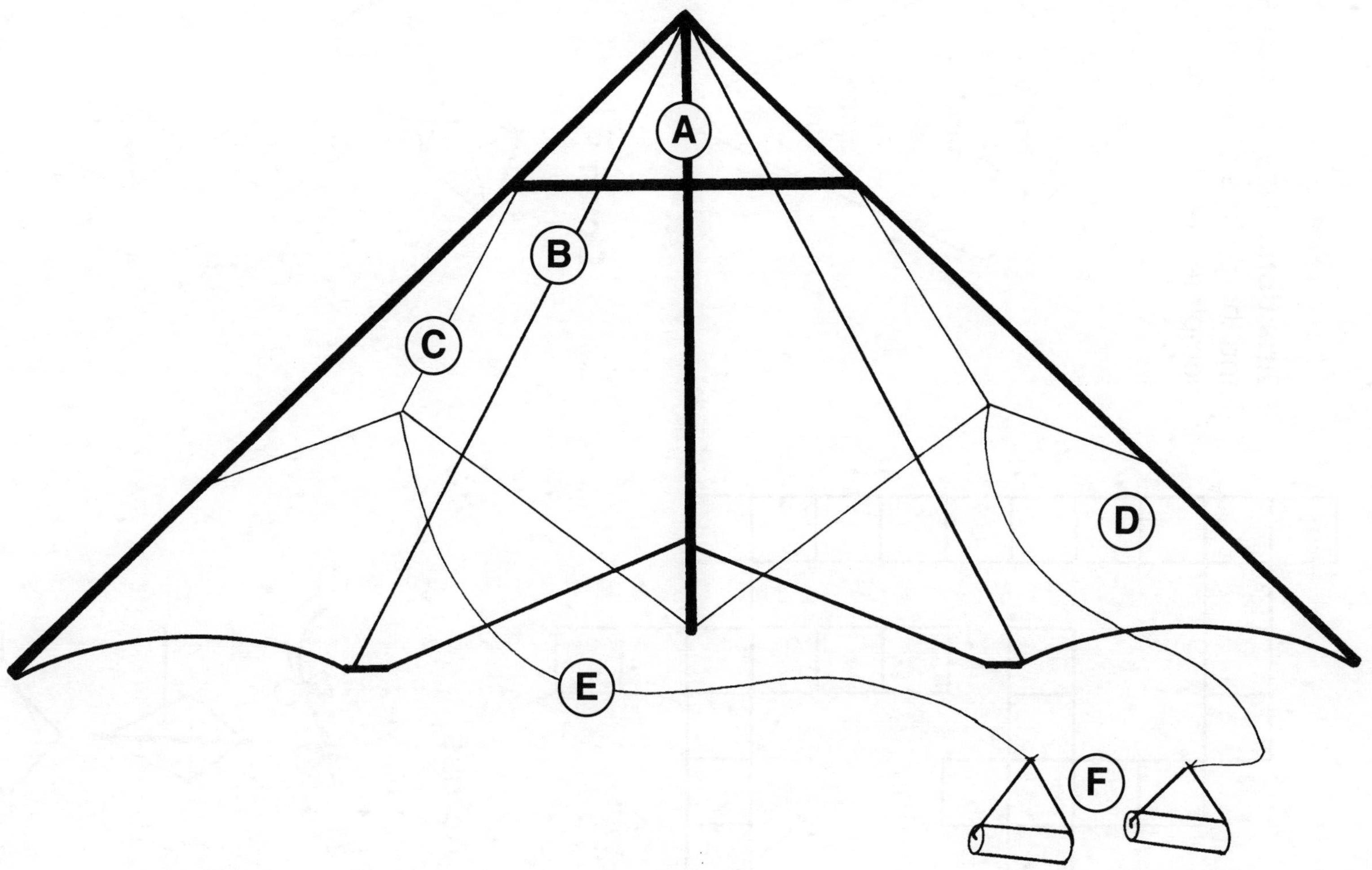

bridle _____   flying line _____   spars _____

cover (skin) _____   handle (spool) _____   spines _____

Parts-of-a-kite Crossword

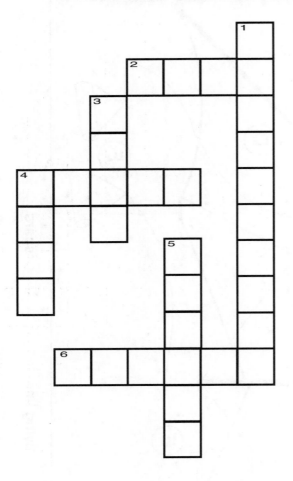

Directions: Use the words in the kite and the picture clues below to complete the crossword.

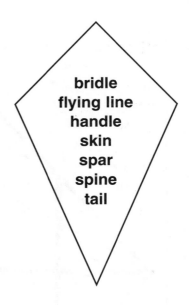

bridle
flying line
handle
skin
spar
spine
tail

Across

 2.

 4.

 6.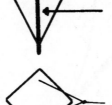

Down

1.

3.

4.

5.

Types-of-kites Crossword

Directions: Use the words in the box and the picture clues below to complete the crossword.

Word Box

box
delta
fighter
flat
parafoil
sled
stunt

Across

3.

5.

6.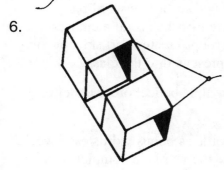

Down

1.

2.

3.

4.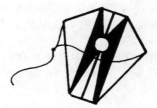

A Kite-flier's Word Bank

Word banks are a great resource for any writing activity. They should be created on chart paper and displayed for all to see and use. Some uses for word banks include:

- ♦ pocket-chart sentences
- ♦ poetry
- ♦ flash cards
- ♦ story writing/personal experiences
- ♦ spelling lists

- ♦ journal writing
- ♦ alphabetical ordering
- ♦ cloze exercises
- ♦ word searches/crossword puzzles
- ♦ dictionary practice

Types of Kites	Parts of a Kite	Adjectives	Verbs	Kite Maneuvers
Bowed	bridle	big	climb	circle
Box	cover	colorful	drift	dive
Cellular	flying line	diamond-shaped	float	drop
Delta	handle	light	fly	figure-eight
Flat	spar	long	glide	land
Sled	spine	square	soar	launch
Soft	tail	triangle		spin
Stunt				turn

Word-bank words can be added to the generated chart as the children become more familiar with the topic.

Here are some high-flying activities:

- After brainstorming kite words, have your children classify like words to form word-bank categories.

- Divide the class into small groups and give each group a card listing four or five word-bank words. (**Note:** The teacher might want to visit each group to ensure that the group members understand the meanings of the words they are using.) Have the groups create short skits or role-plays that utilize their words. The skits or role-plays can then be presented to the class.

- Place your desired word-bank words on index cards; place them in alphabetical order under each appropriate letter on a wall displayed alphabet strip.

- If you give weekly spelling words, use three or four word-bank words as bonus words each week. Ask them to not only know the word's meanings but be able to use the words in complete sentences.

20

A Kite Journal

Directions

1. Using the Kite Cover Pattern (page 22), cut out a construction paper or tagboard cover for each child. Have each child write his her name on the top portion of the kite cover and the journal's title on the bottom portion. Then have the children decorate their covers, attaching ribbon or yarn tails.

2. Reproduce and cut out the desired number of kite writing pages for each child (Kite-writing Patterns, pages 23 and 24).

3. Stack the cut out writing pages; top the pages with a kite cover (page 22). Staple the pages to the cover at the top of each booklet.

4. Have the children write a journal entry daily, including various facts and information they have learned about kites. Also plan to use the prepared booklets to encourage creative writing or free-verse poetry. Here are a few examples:

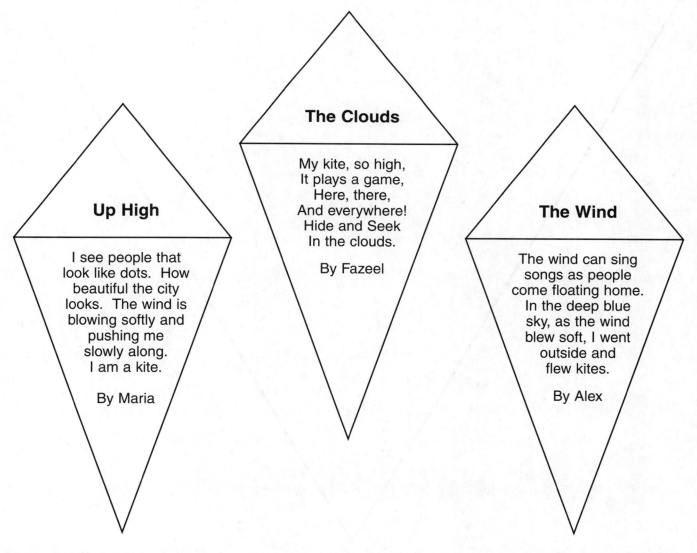

Up High

I see people that look like dots. How beautiful the city looks. The wind is blowing softly and pushing me slowly along. I am a kite.

By Maria

The Clouds

My kite, so high, It plays a game, Here, there, And everywhere! Hide and Seek In the clouds.

By Fazeel

The Wind

The wind can sing songs as people come floating home. In the deep blue sky, as the wind blew soft, I went outside and flew kites.

By Alex

Kite Cover Pattern

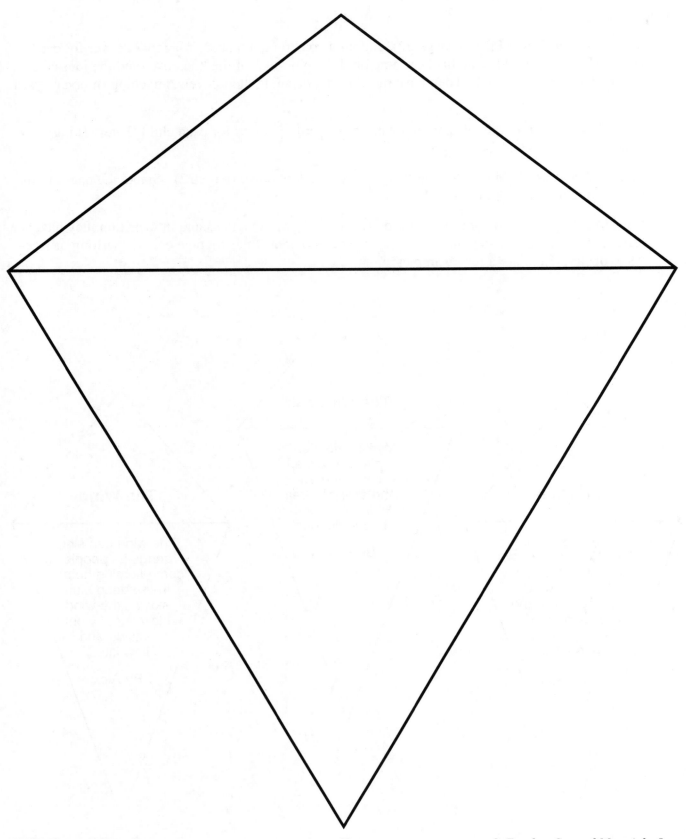

22

Kite-writing Pattern 1

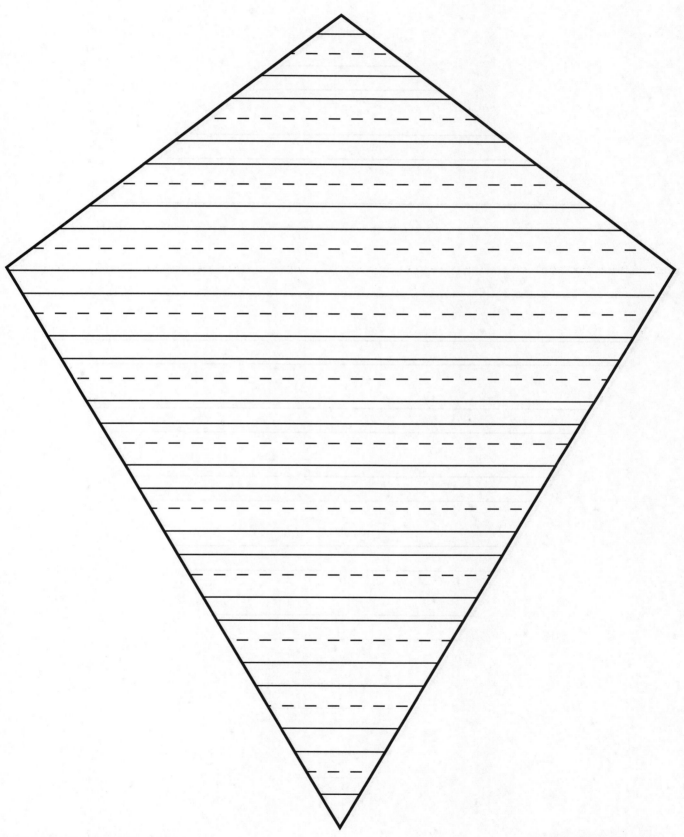

Kite-writing Pattern 2

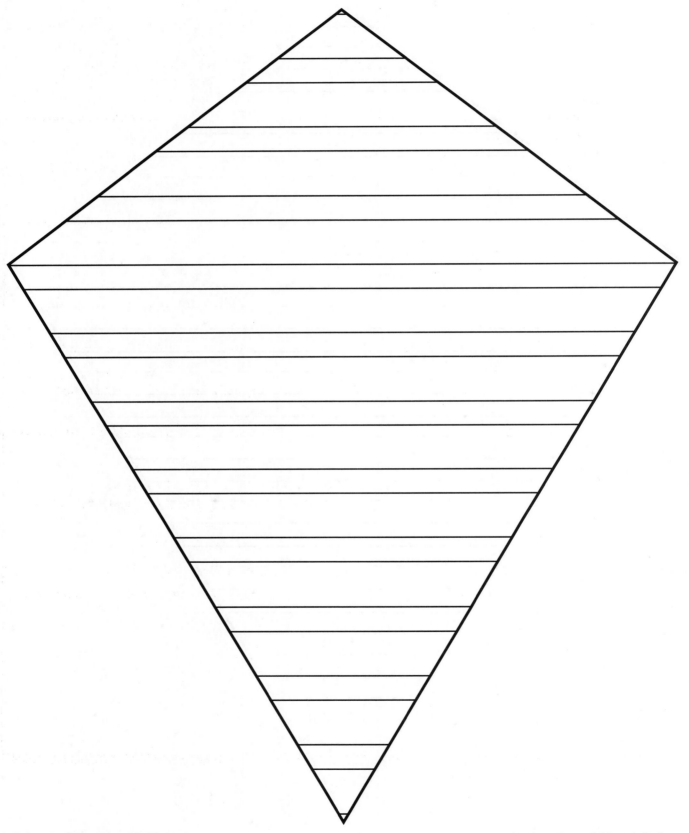

The Emperor and the Kite

By Jane Yolen

Summary

In this award-winning, Caldecott Honor book, tiny Djeow Seow, the youngest child of the emperor, is so small and insignificant that no one notices her. She eats and plays alone, flying her kite every day. Only a monk speaks to her. One day, evil men come and lock the emperor in a tower. All of his sons and daughters are scared and flee the kingdom. Djeow Seow is the only one who stays and helps her father. Every day she flies her kite to send him a basket of food. The monk sees what she is doing and gives her an idea. Djeow Seow uses the idea to help her father escape. When the emperor is free, he realizes how special and valuable his smallest daughter really is.

The outline below is a suggested plan for using various activities that are presented in this unit. You can adapt these ideas to fit your own classroom situation.

Sample Plan

Lesson 1

- Recite the Kite Chants (page 39).
- Sing the Kite Songs (page 40).
- Pre-teach story vocabulary (pages 30–31).
- Read *The Emperor and the Kite.*
- Conduct a class discussion about feelings (page 26, Enjoying the Book, #1).
- Complete Let's Be Choosy (page 32).

Lesson 2

- Recite the Kite Chants (page 39) and sing the Kite Songs (page 40).
- Reread *The Emperor and the Kite.*
- Complete these comprehension activities: Story Questions (page 28) and Tell Me a Story (page 30).
- Enjoy the point-of-view activity (page 27, #1).
- Create character comparisons (page 26, Enjoying the Book, #2).
- Write Haiku poems (page 38).

Lesson 3

- Read about Kites Around the World (page 27, #4).
- Have the children conduct Kite Facts research (page 43).
- Conduct a creative writing experience (page 27, #2).
- Explore some math Flying-line Estimations (page 54).

Lesson 4

- Have the children present their Kite Facts research reports.
- Create kite Word Cards (page 43).
- Make Mini-kites (page 62).
- Begin planning your culminating activities (pages 67 and 68).

Lesson 5

- Enjoy your Class Kite Day (page 67).

Overview of Activities

Setting the Stage
---

1. Singing is a great way to start each day—and get children excited about a theme! Write the Kite Songs (page 40) on flip-chart paper and practice singing a song each day.

2. Enlarge the poems (page 36) and chants (page 39); display them. An alternative is to copy the words onto sentence strips and display them in a pocket chart. Encourage the children to identify rhyming patterns, initial and final consonants of key words, as well as phonics rules, such as silent /gh/, y sounding like long /i/ at the end of words, -ing endings, and -ay sounding like long /a/. Practice context clues by covering up part of a word, or a whole word, and have the children fill in the missing parts.

3. To pre-teach key vocabulary from the story, photocopy page 31 and have the children match the words to their meanings.

4. Ask the children if they have ever felt tiny, small, or unimportant? Have they ever had difficulty getting an adult to listen to them? How could, or did, they solve that problem?

5. Show the children the cover of the book and ask them what an emperor is. What does an emperor do? Ask them in what country they think the story might take place.

Enjoying the Book
---

1. Lead a class discussion on emotions and feelings. Show pictures from the story and ask the children to identify how Djeow Seow and other characters felt. Provide each child with a copy of Feelings (page 29). Have the children discuss, in small groups or as a class, their opinions of the emotions that each character would have felt.

   As an extension, encourage them to brainstorm synonyms for emotion/feeling words. Write these words on cardstock to make an emotions word bank. Encourage them to use these words when completing their daily journal writing or writing creative kite stories (page 34).

2. In terms of size, Djeow Seow and her father, the emperor, are exact opposites. Even though they are opposites in size, they share like qualities (loyalty, bravery, and being wise rulers). Using the comparison chart on page 33, have each child first brainstorm how Djeow Seow and the emperor are different. (**Note:** Possible answers can be found on page 80.) Have them share their ideas in small groups. (**Note:** Encourage the children to record ideas they learn from others on their sheets.) While they are still in small groups, assign the task of brainstorming and recording at least two qualities that both characters share.

Overview of Activities *(cont.)*

Extending the Book

1. To better understand the concept of point-of-view, have your children retell the story, in writing or orally, from the different characters' perspectives, such as the monk, the evil men, the brothers or sisters, or the emperor. Discuss why some of the characters did not notice or value Djeow Seow.

2. Lead the children through a brainstorming time discussing what it would have been like to be Djeow Seow's favorite kite. How would it feel? Where would you fly? What would you see? Depending on your children's writing strengths, have them draft, peer-edit, share their rough draft story ideas, and expand and revise their stories before creating their final copies.

3. Poems are a wonderful way to highlight phonics skills such as rhyming words and phonemic patterns necessary for decoding words. Write the poem *My Kite* (page 37) on flip-chart paper. Read the poem as a whole class, then have the children underline/circle or otherwise highlight language patterns that they can find in the poem, such as the rhyming words or the letter /y/ used as a vowel. Then encourage them to apply their phonetic detective skills to complete page 37.

4. Learn about kites from around the world by using pages 57 and 58 as information sheets. Once your children have read and understood this background information, there are a variety of activities that you can use to build on this theme. Refer to page 43 for a variety of kite-fact activities.

5. Read other kite stories such as *The Berenstain Bears and the Big Red Kite* or *Moonlight Kite* (Bibliography, page 76). Have the children compare the story elements between the two read stories (see page 41). You may also want to use these two stories to extend and reinforce your children's knowledge about types of kites (see the Venn diagram on page 41).

Story Questions

1. What does Djeow Seow's name mean in English?

   _____

2. Why does her father forget that he has a fourth daughter (Djeow Seow)?

   _____

   _____

3. What is her favorite toy?

   _____

4. What did the evil men do?

   _____

   _____

5. How did she keep her father alive?

   _____

   _____

6. How did the emperor escape?

   _____

   _____

   _____

7. Who was the most loyal child now and why?

   _____

   _____

Draw a picture of your favorite part of the story on the back of this paper.

Feelings

Draw a feeling face after each question.

happy **sad** **scared** **worried**

Beginning of Story

1. How does Djeow Seow feel when she plays alone?

2. How do her brothers and sisters feel when they help the emperor?

Middle of Story

3. How does the emperor feel when the evil men capture him and put him in the tower?

4. How does Djeow Seow feel when she sees her father captured?

5. How do her brothers and sisters feel?

End of Story

6. How does the emperor feel when he escapes the tower?

7. How do the evil men feel when they are put in prison?

8. How does Djeow Seow feel when she gets to sit by her father's throne?

Tell Me a Story

Djeow Seow was the (1) _____ child.

She ate and played (2) _____ . One day

(3) _____ men put the emperor in a tall (4) _____ .

Every day Djeow Seow sailed her (5) _____ to his prison window with a

basket of (6) _____ . The old (7) _____ gave her an

idea. Djeow Seow made a (8) _____ rope. She flew her kite to the

window and the emperor (9)_____ down the rope. Then the emperor

threw the evil men in (10)_____ The emperor

(11)_____ his kingdom with Djeow Seow close by his side.

She (12) _____ her father. She ruled the kingdom after he became old.

Word Bank

prison	smallest	ruled	alone
loved	food	tower	monk
kite	long	evil	slid

Word Match

Draw a line to match the word to its meaning.

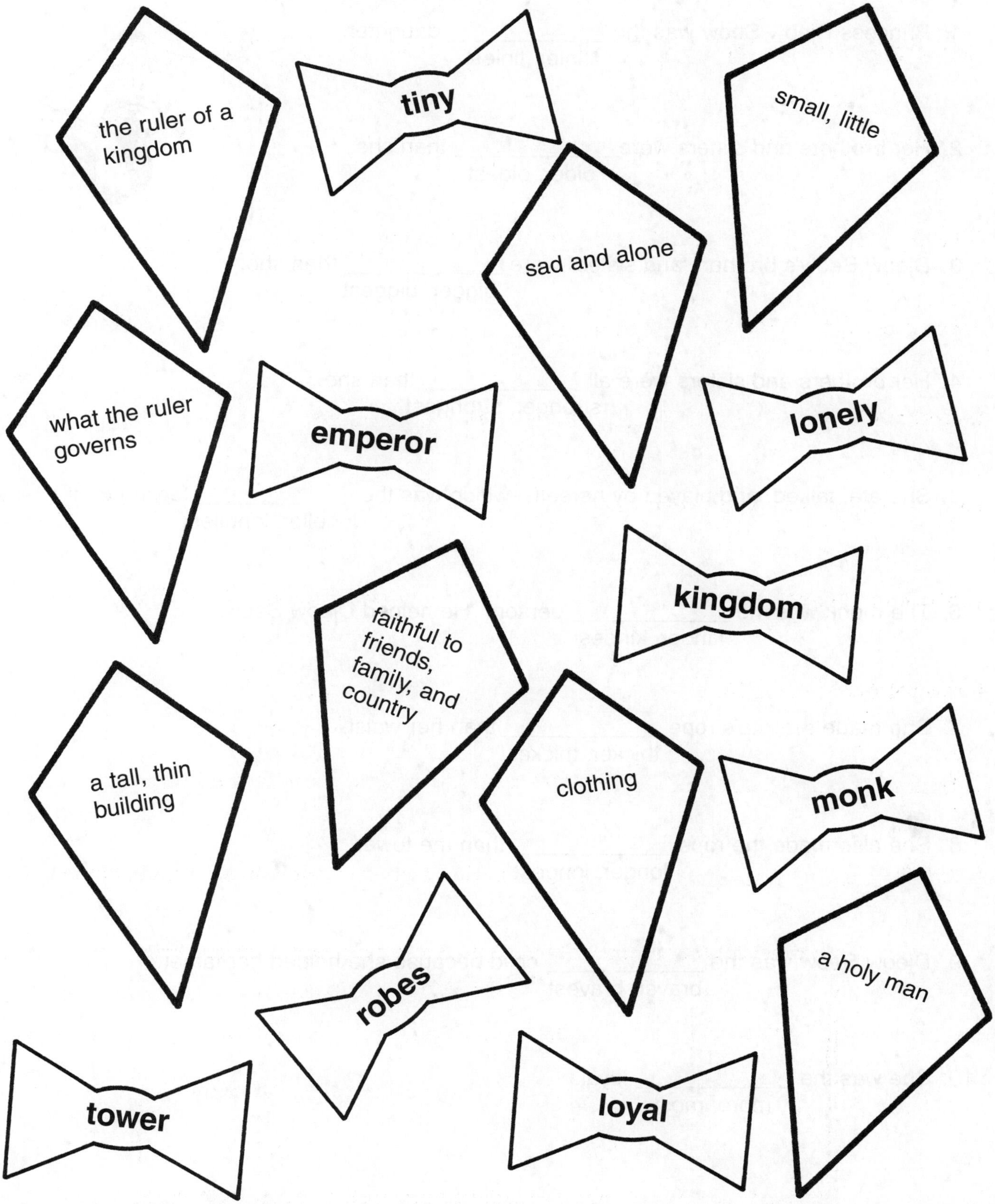

the ruler of a kingdom

tiny

small, little

sad and alone

what the ruler governs

emperor

lonely

faithful to friends, family, and country

kingdom

a tall, thin building

clothing

monk

robes

a holy man

tower

loyal

Let's Be Choosy

Choose the correct word. Write it on the blank line.

1. Princess Djeow Seow was the _____ daughter.
   tinier, tiniest

2. Her brothers and sisters were _____ than she.
   older, oldest

3. Djeow Seow's brothers and sisters were _____ than she.
   bigger, biggest

4. Her brothers and sisters were all _____ than she.
   stronger, strongest

5. She ate, talked, and played by herself—which was the _____ feeling of all.
   lonelier, loneliest

6. The monk was the _____ person. He helped Djeow Seow.
   kinder, kindest

7. She made the kite's rope _____ than her waist.
   thicker, thickest

8. She also made the rope _____ than the tower.
   longer, longest

9. Djeow Seow was the _____ child because she helped her father.
   braver, bravest

10. She was the _____ loyal.
    more, most

Dare to Compare

The Emperor

Djeow Seow

How they were the same ←

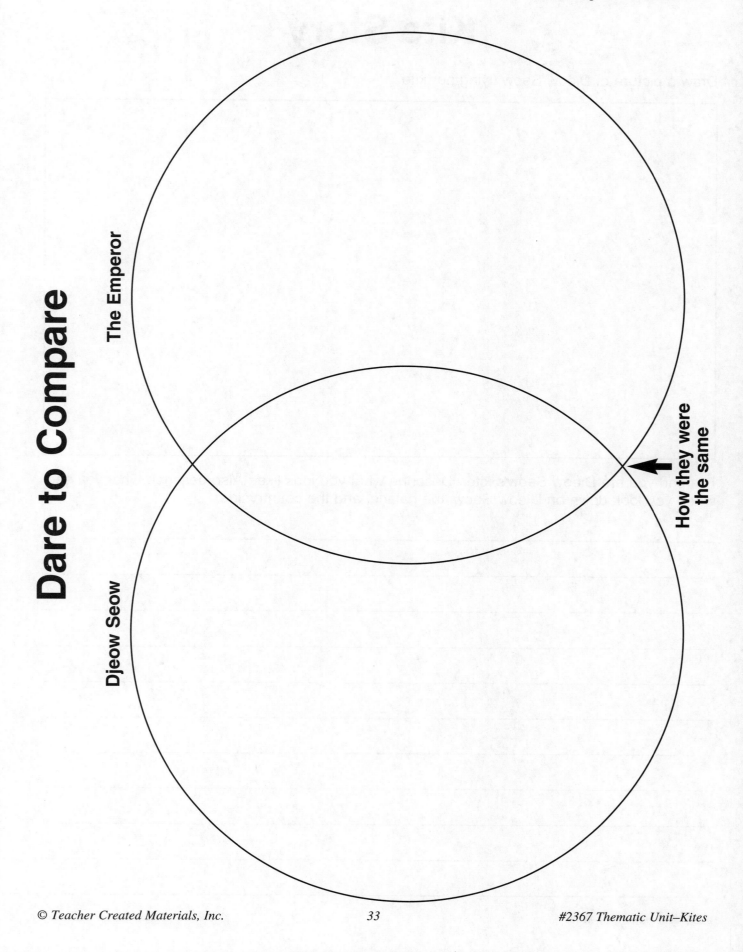

Kite Story

Draw a picture of Djeow Seow flying her kite.

Pretend you are Djeow Seow's kite. Describe what you look like. Also describe what you see when you look down on Djeow Seow, the palace, and the countryside.

_____

_____

_____

_____

_____

_____

_____

_____

_____

_____

_____

Writing Experiences

Journal Writing

Written and oral language expression are an important part of a child's development, therefore, journal writing should be recognized as personal scripting. When reading your children's writings, you should be giving positive feedback with little, if any, criticism of writing skill abilities. Writing topics may include interesting kite facts learned, experiences with kites, summaries of activities completed during the kite unit, summaries of books read or researched, and interesting information about kites around the world.

A kite cover pattern is provided on page 22. Make a copy for each child. Reproduce the desired writing pages (pages 23 and 24) to use as inside pages. (**Note:** The cover pattern and writing pages can also be enlarged and used for creating a class big book.)

Sequencing Language

Your children will need to use sequencing skills in order to teach each other kite-flying skills or maneuvers. Using generated vocabulary words (Glossary, page 75), have your children write their own versions of how to build and/or launch a specific type of kite; for example, a Sled kite.

Parts of a kite	Safety	Launching/Flying/Landing
spine	courteous	lift
spar	power lines	trim
skin	storm	wind speed

Story Mapping

A story map is a graphic organizer that helps teach the elements of a story: the title, author, setting, characters, problems, events, and solutions to the problems. Choose a fictional book from the Bibliography (pages 76 and 77) and read the story to your class. Then, using a large sheet of paper, create a story map based on the reading.

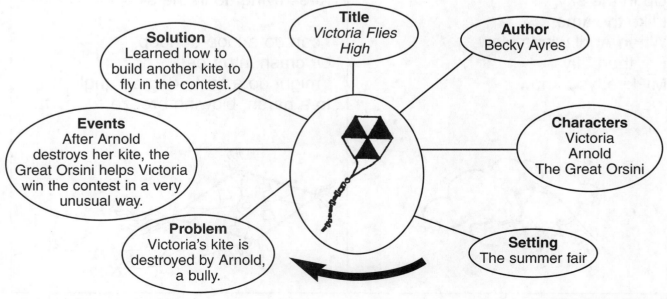

Title *Victoria Flies High*

Author Becky Ayres

Solution Learned how to build another kite to fly in the contest.

Events After Arnold destroys her kite, the Great Orsini helps Victoria win the contest in a very unusual way.

Characters Victoria Arnold The Great Orsini

Problem Victoria's kite is destroyed by Arnold, a bully.

Setting The summer fair

Kite Poetry

by Larissa Sampson

Kite Days

A kite, a sky, and a good firm
  breeze,
Acres of ground—away from trees,
One hundred yards of clean, strong
  string,
Oh boy, oh boy! I call this spring!

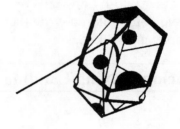

Dream

I often sit and wish that I
Could be a kite up in the sky,
And ride upon the breeze and go
Whichever way I chanced to blow.

My Kite

My kite can fly
So high, so high,
'Tis like a speck
Up in the sky,
I like the time
When April winds blow,
For then I fly
My kite, you know.

Kites

Oh, how I'd like to be a kite,
To fly up really high.
Yes, that's the life,
Kites flying up in the sky.

I can do a loop-de-loop,
Or crash into trees.
I might do a thirty-degree angle,
In a harsh, blowing breeze.

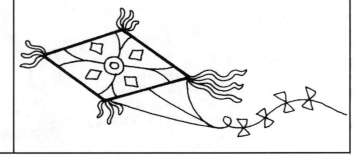

My Kite

My kite can fly
So high, so high,
'Tis like a speck
Up in the sky,
I like the time
When April winds blow,
For then I fly
My kite, you know.

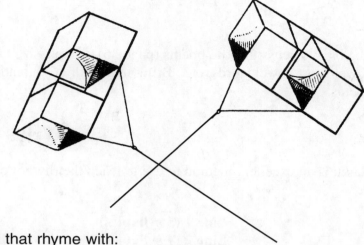

Read the poem. Find words in the poem that rhyme with:

• try   _____   _____   _____   _____

          _____

• grow   _____   _____

• deck   _____

• dime   _____

• bite   _____

• cup   _____

• bike   _____

Read the poem again. Search for these words:

1. 'ow' says long-o sound   _____   _____

2. 'y' says long-i sound   _____   _____   _____

3. long-i sound with a silent e   _____   _____   _____

4. the fourth month of the year   _____

Read-Write-Listen

Read

Read and discuss the kite poems (page 36). Emphasize language skills such as rhyming words, long vowel/short vowel words, etc. Bring the children's attention to the rhythm of the language in the poems.

Write

Haiku is an excellent method to use to teach the rhythm of the English language.

Line 1 (5 syllables)	**Kites are wonderful**
Line 2 (7 syllables)	**Diving, soaring, and floating**
Line 3 (5 syllables)	**Way up in the sky**

Make a poetry big book. Begin by having your children write and illustrate kite poems, either individually or cooperatively. Glue copies of the children's poetry and illustrations on pages of construction paper. Using an actual kite skin or a piece of rip-stop nylon, cover two pieces of stiff cardboard for the booklet's cover; title the booklet: *High Flying Poetry.*

Listen

Compare and contrast two of the kite poems (page 36), emphasizing the poems' style and/or content.

Have the children listen to the following chant poem:

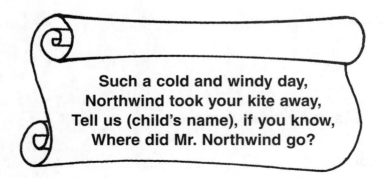

Such a cold and windy day,
Northwind took your kite away,
Tell us (child's name), if you know,
Where did Mr. Northwind go?

Ask them to sit in a circle. Choose one child to sit in the middle with his or her eyes closed. Place a small kite behind his or her back. Have all the remaining children say the first two lines of the poem. Have a child pretend to be the Northwind and take the kite from behind the child's back and return to his or her place. The child then places the kite behind his or her back. Everyone then says the last two lines of the poem. The child in the center opens his or her eyes and tries to guess who has taken the kite by asking, "Have you taken my kite, (a child's name)?" The questioned child answers, "Yes," or "No." The game continues with a new child (the one who took the kite) in the middle.

Kite Chants

I am a **Dragon** kite.
My tail is very long.
I twist and turn with style and grace.
I am very strong!

I am a **Bowed** kite.
I don't need a tail.
My curved spar catches the wind.
It lets me fly so well!

I am a big **Box** kite.
I love all types of air.
My open shape can catch the wind,
And fly most anywhere!

I am a **Fighter** kite.
I swoop and dive and spin.
I try to cut others' strings,
So I can win, win, win!

I am a **Stunt** kite.
I need two lines to fly.
Pull my strings to spin and loop.
You'll love me—give it a try!

I am a simple **Sled** kite.
Just sticks, plastic, and strings.
I fly high in the lightest breeze.
It's just like having wings!

I am a **Delta** kite.
Three sides and a keel.
I fly in light and strong breezes.
Just hold tight to my reel!

I am a **Soft** kite.
No hardware makes me light.
You can take me anywhere.
Just roll me up real tight!

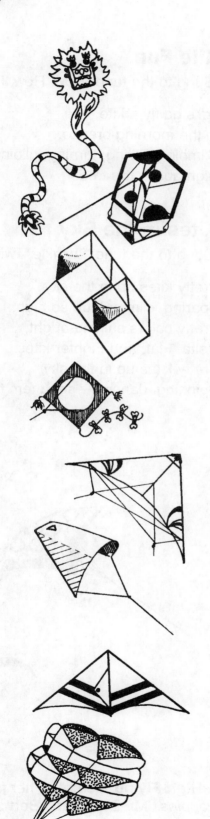

Kite Songs

Kite Fun

(Sung to the tune "Row, Row, Row Your Boat")

Let's go fly a kite,
In the morning breeze.
Climbing, diving, turning, gliding,
High above the trees!

Kites in the Sky

(Sung to the tune "Twinkle, Twinkle Little Star")

Pretty kites up in the sky,
Soaring, climbing up so high.
Pretty colors shining bright,
Delta, Flat, and Fighter kites.
Pretty kites up in the sky,
Spinning, dancing—see them fly!

Go Fly a Kite

(Sung to the tune "Three Blind Mice")

Go fly a kite.
Go fly a kite.
Come out and play.
Come out and play.
All the children run out to fly.
Their kites are high up in the sky.
It's a very nice day to give it a try,
So let's fly a kite.
Oh, let's fly a kite!

A High-Flying Idea: Another famous kite song is "Let's Go Fly a Kite" from the movie *Mary Poppins.* Mr. Banks and Bert sing the song near the end of the movie. The music and lyrics to the song are by Richard M. Sherman and Robert B. Sherman. If possible, allow the children to watch this portion of this classic movie.

Comparing Kite Stories

Using a Venn diagram is a visually meaningful way to compare stories. Two enjoyable kite stories that are suitable for primary-aged children are *Moonlight Kite* by Helen E. Buckley and *The Berenstain Bears and the Big Red Kite* by Stan and Jan Berenstain.

After reading and discussing the two stories, help the children compare the stories by drawing a Venn diagram on the chalkboard or chart paper. Encourage the children to share their thoughts and record them on the Venn diagram.

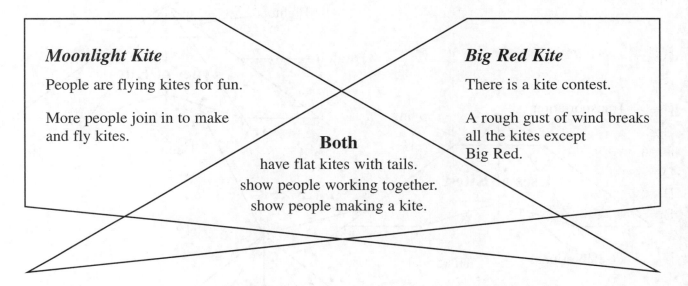

Moonlight Kite

People are flying kites for fun.

More people join in to make and fly kites.

Big Red Kite

There is a kite contest.

A rough gust of wind breaks all the kites except Big Red.

Both
have flat kites with tails.
show people working together.
show people making a kite.

Venn diagrams can also be used to compare more specific elements of the two stories, or elements within one story. For example, in *Moonlight Kite* the characters of Nicholas and Carlos can be compared as follows:

Nicholas...
   is a boy.
   is a student.
   lives in a village.

Both...
   like flying kites.
   were happy when other
   people flew their kites.

Carlos...
   is a man.
   is a monk.
   lives in a monastery.

Your Venn diagrams can also be completed using a type-of-kite theme. For example, in *The Bernstain Bears and the Big Red Kite* several types of kites are shown. After the children have studied several types of kites, a kite-shaped comparison chart can be made.

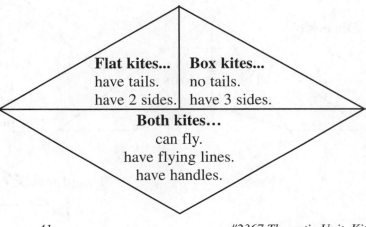

Flat kites...
have tails.
have 2 sides.

Box kites...
no tails.
have 3 sides.

Both kites...
can fly.
have flying lines.
have handles.

Kite Mapping

Another helpful language tool is an information map. It is a helpful tool for brainstorming fiction or nonfiction writing.

Have the children research information about types of kites, parts of a kite, uses of kites, and descriptions of kites. Then build an informational map on chart paper; display. Here is one example of a completed map:

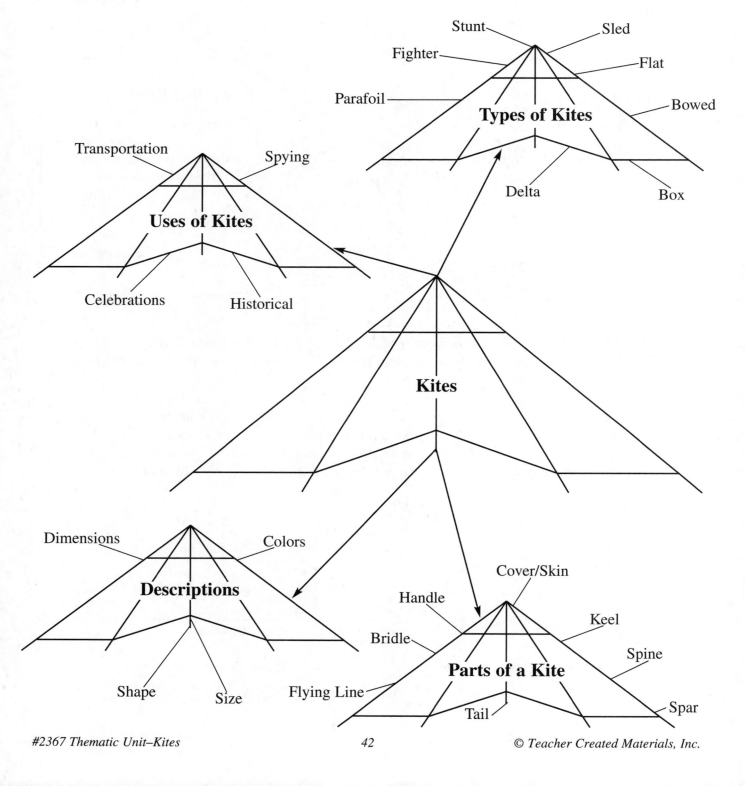

Word Cards

After reading a fiction or nonfiction kite selection to your children (Bibliography, pages 76 and 77), discuss the book and have them recall some of the kite words heard. Using chart paper or writing on a chalkboard, list these words. Distribute Kite Word Cards sheets (page 44) to each child. Have them copy and illustrate the words of their choice (or ones you have selected). Have them cut out their cards and keep them in a word-cards folder. (A file folder that has been stapled or taped along its right and left sides works well.) New word cards can be added to the folder periodically. As your unit of study continues, the folders can be brought out and practiced.

Another way to encourage vocabulary, is to explore some kite facts (see below) and create word cards appropriate to knowledge gained.

Kite Facts

During the introductory stage of your *Kites* unit, display nonfiction book titles (Bibliography, page 77) in a center area. Have the children look through and/or read the books. At this point, encourage them to focus on what they find interesting about kites, as well as what they want to learn about them.

Distribute a Kite Facts sheet (page 45) to each child. Have them work alone or in small groups to list kite facts that they found particularly interesting. Have them write and correctly illustrate a *specific* fact (e.g., a fact statement pertaining to handles or spools of a kite should not show the whole kite). After the children share their facts with fellow classmates; display their fact sheets.

As you move through your *Kites* unit, periodically provide new Kite Facts sheets. Have them write and illustrate their latest facts. At the end of your unit, a display of the Kite Facts sheets will make an excellent visual record of what they have learned. **Note:** This activity is a good lead-in or follow-up to creating a KWL chart (page 8).

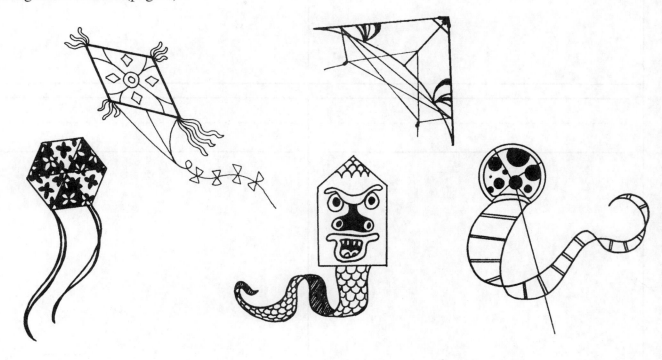

Kite Word Cards

44

Kite Facts

Name	
_____	
Date	**My kite fact is...**
_____	_____
	_____

Name	
_____	
Date	**My kite fact is...**
_____	_____
	_____

Kite Word Search

A high-flying reminder: words can be diagonal, backwards, and, of course, forwards.

```
N P N O R T S T R I N G A W L U
L I O T M J Z O E U T W L O G I
Q A I I A F O L A R Z R C P P Q
D M Y U W I G F Q R M A O G Y L
E Z J O D N S R O A S W L P O L
C C L S A I L G C P J O O F V D
O B D I P B A Z M R R S R B O I
R V R Y M E Z M D I F I F K Q V
A T B I V Q C Y O L X U U U G E
T U L H W H L K K N Q N L W D H
I C J B R I G H T Y D D S N D I
O X P O E D O F C R O R I Y L G
N R P P Y R Z U Z T E W K I B H
S H W L B R E E Z E S S A S R B
Z I F A E E Z Z U R A S E S V U
T A I L S L N S Q U A R E M O D
```

Word Search Bank

April	diamond	soars
blow	dip	speck
breeze	dive	square
bright	fly	string
climb	high	tails
colorful	sail	triangle
decorations	sky	wind

Wind Movement

Go outside. Use your senses to see, hear, feel, and smell the wind.

I saw...	
I heard...	
I felt...	
I smelled...	

How's the Weather?

Using the Beaufort scale, estimate how strong the wind is. Record your observations for one week and then decide when it is the best time of day to fly a kite.

Beaufort Scale

Code Number	Description	Signs
0	Calm	Calm; no wind movement
1	Light air	Smoke drifts; dry leaves rustle; few kites fly
2	Light breeze	Wind felt on face; tree leaves rustle; most kites fly
3	Gentle breeze	Light flags blow; tree leaves and twigs move all the time; kites fly well
4	Moderate breeze	Small branches move; papers blow; dust is raised; some kites crash
5	Fresh breeze	Small trees sway; strong waves on lakes; kite strings break
6	Strong breeze	Large branches move; umbrella used with difficulty; kites break

	Beginning Of The School Day	After Morning Recess	After Lunch
Monday			
Tuesday			
Wednesday			
Thursday			
Friday			

The best time of day to fly a kite is _____ because the wind is usually _____ .

Kite Safety

A kite is actually a wing. Its ability to fly is affected by both the wind conditions and the kite's design. Wind causes a lifting effect on the top surface of the kite as well as a simultaneous upward thrust against the lower surface of the kite. When these two forces are balanced or nearly equal, a kite remains afloat in the air.

Activities to Reinforce Kite Safety

1. Present the kite-safety rules (below). Then have the children brainstorm additional safety rules. Keep a record of all of the kite rules on flip-chart paper.

2. Discuss what safe places and safe weather mean to kite fliers.

3. Reproduce, cut out, and assemble the Kite-safety Minibook (pages 50–53), one per child. Read and discuss each page. Allow time for the children to color the pages. Have them take home the completed books to share kite-safety information with their families.

4. Divide the class into small groups and have them role-play the events and solutions to various kite-flying problems they might encounter. You may then choose a few of these to be presented to the entire class.

Kite-safety Rules

- Don't fly your kite in wet or stormy weather.

- Never fly your kite near power lines—most kites can conduct electricity.

- Do not fly your kite near streets, roads, or bike paths.

- Keep your kite away from trees—if you fly too close to trees, your kite could become tangled or ripped.

- Be careful of dangers on the ground—you don't want to fall into or over anything.

- Fly your kite away from people who are walking or riding bikes.

- Choose a hazard-free, open space to fly your kite.

- Learn how to judge the wind and keep control of your kite at all times.

- Never leave your kite unattended.

- If you are flying your kite with other kite fliers, spread out to avoid getting your flying lines tangled.

- Be courteous and use common sense—this is the most important kite rule to remember!

Kite Safety Minibook

_____

Name

I fly my kite safely because I stay away from danger.

1

Kite Safety Minibook *(cont.)*

I stay away from trees. Trees "eat" kites.

2

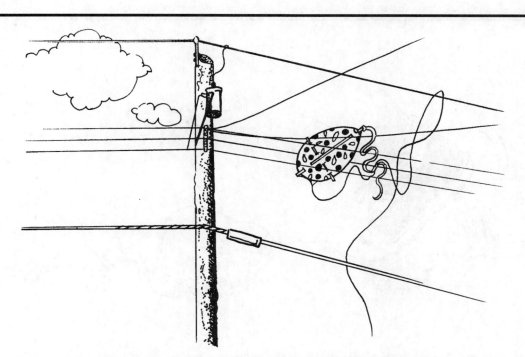

I stay away from power lines. Power lines are dangerous.

3

Kite Safety Minibook *(cont.)*

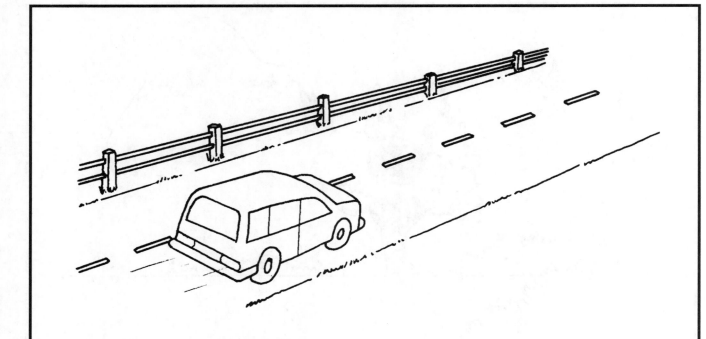

I stay away from people and roads.

4

I watch for holes and big rocks.

5

Kite Safety Minibook *(cont.)*

I never fly my kite in wet or stormy weather.

6

I have fun when I fly my kite safely.

7

Flying-line Estimation

This is an excellent exercise to utilize when conducting an introductory or review lesson on measurement. Estimation means making an educated guess. Have the children practice estimating skills by predicting the length of a kite's flying line. (**Note:** Longer flying lines can be used for older children, shorter flying lines for younger children.) Using a benchmark and modeling a few estimation activities will help give your children a frame of reference for generating accurate estimations.

Place a ruler and an equal length of flying line beside it. Put a card reading: "This is 12 inches." ("This is 30 cm.") next to the ruler. This is the benchmark length. Beside the ruler place a longer length of loosely looped flying line. After studying the benchmark, have each child estimate how long the looped flying line is. Write each child's estimation on a piece of chart paper or an enlarged, posted kite pattern (pages 70 and 71). When all the children have made an estimate, use the benchmark ruler to measure the looped flying line to determine its length.

This estimation activity can easily be adapted to measure the sides of a kite skin, spines, spars, etc. It also provides an excellent language opportunity for reviewing introduced kite-parts vocabulary.

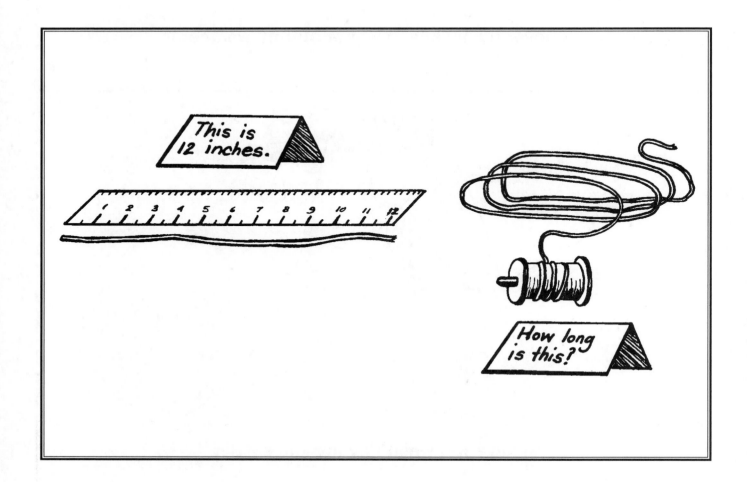

I Spy!

Delta Kite

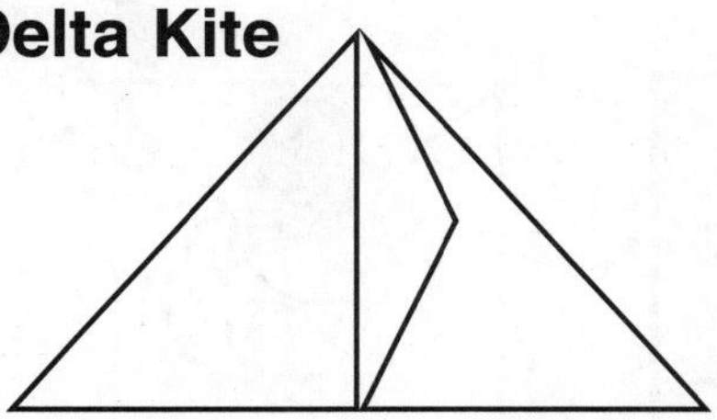

I see: ___4___ ‿‿triangles‿‿ △
shape

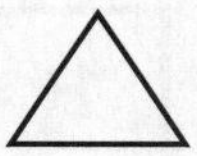

Sled Kite

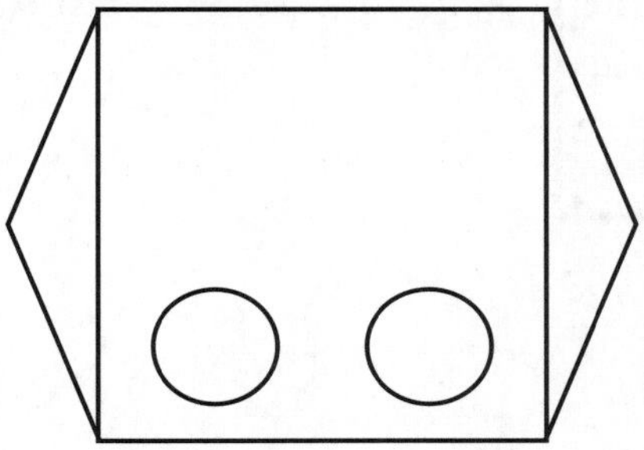

I see: _____ _____ ◯
shape

I see: _____ _____ △
shape

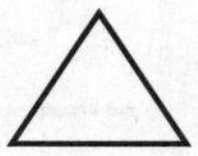

I see: _____ _____ ☐
shape

Korean Fighter Kite

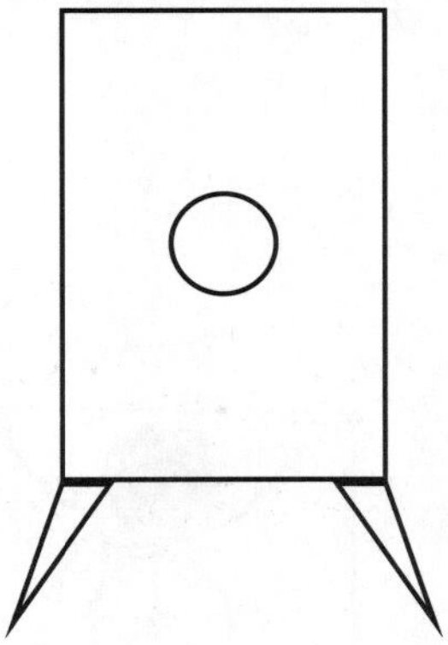

I see: _____ _____ ◯
shape

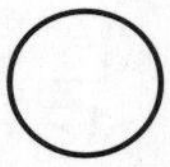

I see: _____ _____ ▭
shape

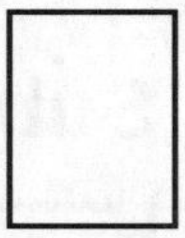

I see: _____ _____ △
shape

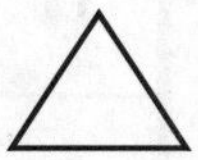

Flat Kite

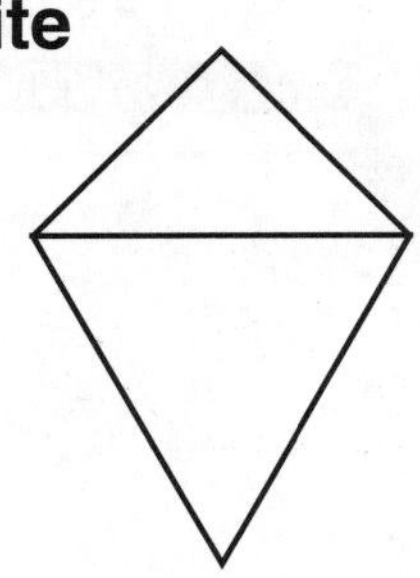

I see: _____ _____ ◇
shape

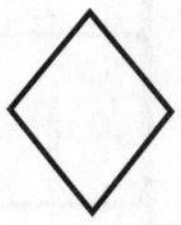

I see: _____ _____ △
shape

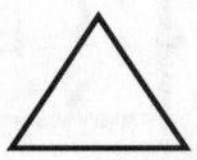

Shape Bank

circle   square   rectangle   triangle   diamond

Break the Code!

Addition

H $7 + 5 =$	**S** $8 + 7 =$
T $4 + 9 =$	**G** $5 + 3 =$
O $7 + 7 =$	**A** $9 + 2 =$
E $8 + 9 =$	**K** $6 + 3 =$
R $3 + 7 =$	**I** $7 + 9 =$

$\overline{}\ \overline{}\ \overline{}\quad\overline{}\ \overline{}\ \overline{}\quad\overline{}\ \overline{}\ \overline{}\ \overline{}\ \overline{}\quad\overline{}\ \overline{}\ \overline{}\ \overline{}$

15 17 17   13 12 17   9 16 13 17 15   15 14 11 10

$\overline{}\ \overline{}\ \overline{}\ \overline{}$!

12 16 8 12

Subtraction

U $9 - 2 =$	**K** $5 - 5 =$
S $10 - 2 =$	**A** $7 - 3 =$
R $6 - 4 =$	**F** $4 - 1 =$
T $8 - 3 =$	**E** $10 - 1 =$
I $9 - 3 =$	**N** $3 - 2 =$

$\overline{}\ \overline{}\ \overline{}\ \overline{}\ \overline{}\quad\overline{}\ \overline{}\ \overline{}\quad\overline{}\ \overline{}\ \overline{}$!

0 6 5 9 8   4 2 9   3 7 1

Kites Around the World

Kite-flying is an ancient sport. No one is sure who invented the kite. Some believe a Greek man named Archytas invented it in 400 B.C. Others believe that about 2000 years ago, kites were invented by the Chinese. Some historians say the Egyptians were the first kite-makers because anthropologists have found old stone carvings showing figures of Egyptian men holding lines connected to objects in the air.

Traders traveling to Asia introduced kite-flying to Europe in the 1400s. By the 1700s, kites could be found all over Europe, but were mainly used as children's toys.

Kite flying is popular in many countries around the world. It is popular with all ages, too. Celebrations involving kites are found in China, Korea, Thailand, Japan, India, and Indonesia. There are many kite competitions and festivals held in various cities throughout the world. The following list tells where some of these kite festivals and competitions are held:

- The *Weifang Festival*, China (April)

- The *Kite Festival*, Japan (May)

- The *Wildwood Kite Festival*, New Jersey, USA (Memorial Day Weekend)

- The *Bali Kite Festival*, Padang Galak Kite Yard, Sanur Beach, Bali (July)

- The *Oirsbeek Kite Festival*, Holland (August)

- The *Bristol Competition*, United Kingdom (September, even-numbered years)

- The *World Cup*, Colombia, South America (December)

Here are a few kite designs and brief explanations of other kite festivals:

Japan

In Japan, Children's Day is celebrated on May 5. The family flies a fish kite from a pole in front of its house for each boy in the family. (**Note:** The girls have recognition other than kites flying in their honor.)

Japanese Fish Kite

Kites Around the World *(cont.)*

India

Makar Sankranti (January 14) is a festival celebrated throughout India. Kite flying and kite fighting are this holiday's highlights. When fighting with kites, the flying line is coated with crushed glass to cut an opponent's line.

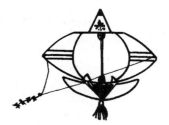

Indian Fighter Kite

China

In China, the ninth day of the ninth month is known as Kites Day or the Festival of Ascending on High. It is traditional for people of all ages to come together and fly kites on that day.

Chinese Kite

Thailand

In Thailand, two types of kites are flown (a large, star-shaped one and a smaller, diamond-shaped one) during the monsoon season to "blow the rains away." The large kite (male) is called the Chula and the smaller kite (female) is called the Pakpao.

These kites are also flown in an annual fighting competition to celebrate the arrival of spring.

Pakpao

Chula

Korea

Many Koreans enjoy kite flying, especially on major holidays such as Ch'usok (August 14–16) and the Lunar New Year Seol-nal (January 1). The traditional Korean kite (Yon) is made with bamboo and paper.

Yon

58

Kite Inventions and Uses

China

In centuries past, kites were used as military weapons to spy on enemies and to find enemy hideouts. Large kites transported people and weapons during battles. One time, when a Chinese emperor was captured, his soldiers flew a huge kite over the prison. The emperor grasped the ropes hanging from the big kite and flew to freedom.

New Zealand

In 1990 Peter Lynn started designing and selling kite "buggies" that looked like tricycles. A kite was attached to the buggy and towed the buggy while the driver steered with his or her feet.

Italy

In the 1500s Leonardo Da Vinci designed plans using kites to fly cables across rivers to help build bridges.

In 1901 Guglielmo Marconi, the inventor of the wireless telegraph, used a kite to lift an antenna 146 yards (135 meters) into the sky. It was used to receive the first radio signal ever transmitted across the ocean—from England to Newfoundland, Canada.

Canada

In 1847 a 10-year-old boy, Homan Walsh, successfully flew a string-toting kite across some water falls. The string was then used to pull stronger ropes, and finally, steel cables were pulled across the falls, which were used to make a bridge.

America

In 1749 Alexander Wilson and Thomas Melville attached thermometers to kites to record the temperature of air at higher altitudes. This is the first recorded attempt to use kites to obtain scientific data.

In June, 1752 Benjamin Franklin and his son attached a wire to the top of a kite and tied a key onto the flying line near the handle. They then went outside to fly the kite during a thunderstorm. When lightning struck the wire it conducted electricity to the key. This helped prove that lightning was a form of electricity.

In 1903 the Wright brothers actually used a kite-glider as their first plane. It was large enough to carry an engine.

Currently, the National Weather Service operates kite-weather stations to measure humidity and temperatures at different heights and with varying wind speeds.

Kite Activities and Facts

Involve your children in some or all of the following activities that reinforce the introduced "Kites Around the World" information:

- Research the similarities and differences of kites from various countries

- Read a variety of kite books from various cultures (Bibliography, pages 76 and 77)

- Keep a record of the shapes and styles of kites from various countries

- Write a story about a favorite design or shape of kite from another country; give some background information as well as illustrate the kite

- Make a graph on flip-chart paper of the various kite celebrations

- Keep a record of the similarities and differences of kite celebrations

- Discover where and when kite festivals are held

- Attend a kite festival or create your own kite celebration

- Work in cooperative groups to discover how and when kites came to Europe and North America

- Research what has been invented as a result of using kites

- Keep a record of famous inventors that used kites as a part of their inventions

- Using globes and world maps, mark locations with flag markers where kites are commonly found and used

- Contact local kite associations, if available, to conduct a workshop or demonstration (Resources, page 78)

Amazing Kite Facts

- In April, 1976 Kazuhiko Asaba of Japan flew 1,050 kites on one single line—a world record!

- In 1979 Steve Flack, a 17-year-old from New York, flew a train of seven kites to a record altitude of over 7.5 miles (12 kilometers) above the ground.

- The smallest kite is smaller than a postage stamp and is flown by thin strands of thread.

- The largest kite in the world is flown each year in a small village near Tokyo, Japan. Its approximate dimensions are 32 feet x 520 feet (10 meters x 16 meters) about the size of a tennis court! It weighs close to 2200 lbs. (1000 kilograms) and has 200 bridle lines, each measuring about 1.5" (4 cm) thick. It takes fifty or more people to fly this incredible kite!

Pinwheel Kite

Materials

- paper (cardboard or tagboard)
- markers or crayons
- scissors
- long straight pin or push pin
- pencil with eraser
- ruler

Directions

1. Cut a 6" (15 cm) square piece of cardboard or tagboard.

2. Decorate the square using the markers or crayons.

3. Draw two diagonal lines to adjoining corners with the pencil and the ruler.

4. Cut along the diagonal lines to within 1" (2.54 cm) of the center.

5. Bend each of the four corners toward the middle—overlapping them at the center point so that they will be able to be pinned together.

6. Push a pin through all four tips. Stick the pin into an eraser on the end of a pencil. (**Note:** Make certain there is enough room on the pin to allow free movement of the pinwheel.)

1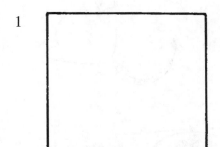

2

3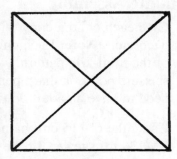

4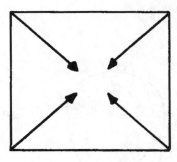

5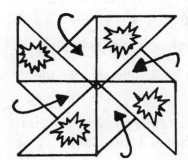

6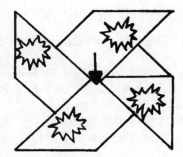

A High-Flying Idea: Experiment with different sizes of pinwheels and compare them to see which one spins the fastest.

Mini-kite

Mini-kites are more for decoration than flying. They are constructed just like a full-sized kite, allowing the children a greater understanding of a kite's structure. A hanging display of these kites is a beautiful sight to see. (**Note:** Be aware that extra adult helpers are necessary for the final stages of construction.)

Materials (per child)

- reproduced kite pattern (page 63), on tagboard
- felt markers, crayons, colored pencils, or stickers
- 2 small pieces of transparent tape
- scissors
- one each 5" (13 cm) and 6" (15 cm) bamboo skewers (kite's spar and spine)
- 10" (25 cm) length of thread (kite's bridle)
- 36" (91 cm) of thread—anchored to and wrapped around a 3" x 5" (8 cm x 13 cm) index card (kite's flying line and handle)
- 3" x ½" (8 cm x 1.3 cm) strip of paper ribbon, colored paper, tissue paper, or crepe paper (kite's tail)

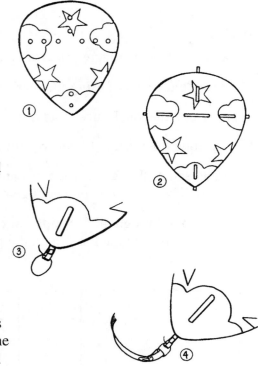

Mini-kite Assembly

1. Give each child a copy of the kite design to cut out and decorate. (**Note:** Each child needs to decorate both sides of the mini-kite pattern.). Punch out the 10 holes with the scissors point or sharp pencil tip. (Younger children will need to have an adult do this for them.)

2. Using the 6" (15 cm) bamboo skewer for the spine and the 5" (13 cm) skewer for the spar, weave the skewers in and out of the holes.

3. Cut a small piece of thread from the flying line and form a loop. Attach this loop with a piece of transparent tape to the bottom of the spine by tying it into tight knots.

4. Draw the ribbon (tail) through the loop and tape in place.

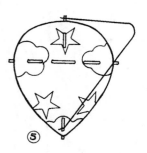

5. Create the bridle by attaching the bridle thread to the top and bottom of the kite's spine.

6. Attach the flying-line thread to the bridle about 4" (10 cm) from the top of the kite by tying it into a small knot.

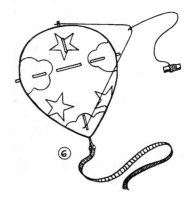

Mini-kite Pattern

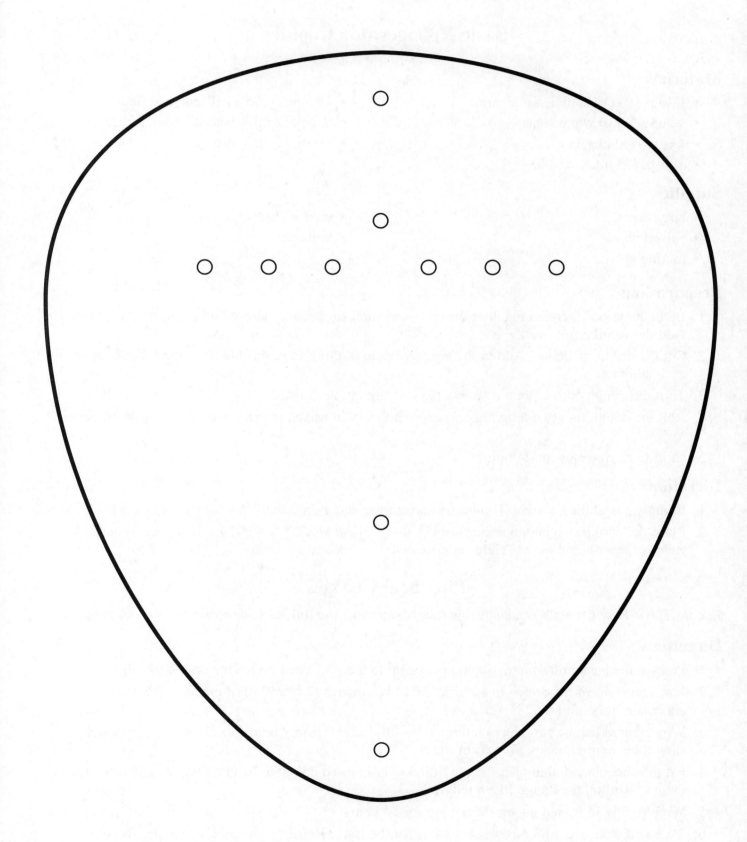

Crazy Cookies

Basic Refrigerator Cookies

Materials

- ¹/₂ cup (100 g) softened margarine
- 1 cup (225 g) white sugar
- 1 egg, well beaten
- 1 tbsp. (15 mL) vanilla

- 1³/₄ cups (375 g) all-purpose flour
- ¹/₂ tsp. (2 mL) baking soda
- ¹/₂ tsp. (2 mL) salt

Supplies

- large bowl
- waxed paper
- mixing spoon

- cookie sheet
- knife

Preparations

1. In the large bowl, cream together the margarine and sugar; add the egg and blend until creamy. Add the vanilla; mix well.
2. Sift the dry ingredients. Add to the sugar mixture in three additions blending the mixture after each addition.
3. Turn the dough onto a floured surface; knead slightly until firm.
4. Roll the dough into two long logs; wrap each firmly in waxed paper. Twist the ends of the paper to seal.
5. Chill in refrigerator for 24 hours.

Directions

1. Remove the chilled dough. Unwrap it and cut the dough into thin ¹/₄" (.6 cm) slices.
2. Place the cookies on an ungreased cookie sheet. Bake at 375° F (190° C) for 10–12 minutes. Remove; cool completely. Yields approximately 90 cookies.

Pinwheel Cookies

Use the Basic Refrigerator Cookies recipe (above) to make the following decorative pinwheel cookies.

Directions

1. Prepare the basic refrigerator cookie recipe up to Step 3. Then divide the dough in half.
2. Place one half of the dough in a bowl. Add two squares (2 oz./50 g) of melted unsweetened chocolate; mix until well blended.
3. With floured hands, pat the remaining half of the dough firmly onto waxed paper. The dough should be approximately ¹/₄" (.6 cm) thick.
4. Pat the chocolate dough over the top of the light-colored dough to form a two-layer slab of cookie dough. Roll up the dough like a jellyroll.
5. Wrap tightly in waxed paper; refrigerate for 24 hours.
6. Slice and bake according to the directions for the Basic Refrigerator Cookies recipe, above.

Crazy Cookies *(cont.)*

Kite Cookies

Materials
- 1 cup (225 g) margarine
- 2½ cups (550 g) all-purpose flour
- 1 tsp. (5 mL) vanilla
- 1 egg (beaten)
- ⅔ cup (150 g) sugar
- ½ tsp. (2 mL) salt
- shortening
- egg yolks
- food coloring

Supplies
- large bowl
- mixing spoon
- cookie sheet
- spatula
- cardboard
- pencil
- scissors
- knife
- new paintbrushes
- cooling rack

Preparations
1. In the large bowl, cream together the margarine and sugar. Add the beaten egg; blend until creamy. Add the vanilla; mix well.
2. Pre-sift the dry ingredients. Add to the sugar mixture in three additions, blending the mixture after each addition.
3. Turn the mixture onto a floured surface; knead slightly until firm.
4. Chill in refrigerator for three to four hours.
5. Remove dough. On lightly floured surface, roll out the dough to approximately a 1" (2.54 cm) thickness.

Directions
1. Make kite patterns (Delta, Star, Triangular, etc.) by first drawing or copying the pattern onto cardboard; cut out each pattern. Slightly grease the patterns with shortening.
2. Lay the cutout patterns (with the greased side down) onto the rolled dough and cut around the kite shapes with the knife.
3. Lift the cookie shape onto the cookie sheet using the spatula.
4. Put one egg yolk in a bowl. Add a desired food-coloring color. (**Note:** Make as many separate bowls of different colors as you'd like.)
5. Using the paintbrushes, draw designs onto the kite-shaped cookies using the egg-yolk paint.
6. Bake at 350° F (180° C) for 8–10 min. Remove from the oven; cool cookies on the cooling rack. Yields approximately 90 cookies.

Web Sites

Use the Internet to gain helpful information about kites. Some interesting Web sites are listed below.

The American Kitefliers Association
www.aka.kite.org

A wealth of information is given including kite building, kite competitions, the art and history of kites, and kite-flying techniques.

Peter's Kite Site
www.win.tue.nl/cs/fm/pp/kites/

This site includes a names-and-picture list plus kite descriptions and links to an amazing number of great kite sites.

Anthony's Kite Workshop
www.sct.gu.edu.au/~anthony/kites/

This site includes a number of plans for building many simple kites.

Kites and Computers
www.kfs.org/kites/simo/kitecomp/kitecomp.html

A great Web site that describes how computers can be used to connect world-wide kite enthusiasts.

The Australian Kitefliers Association
www.moreinfo.com.au/aks/

This Australian Web site provides many links to interesting kite sites.

The Kite Ranch
www.kiteranch.com/index.htm

Links to many useful kite sites are provided.

Kites in the Classroom
www.island.net/~kitebike/index.htm

Kite making, kite decorating, and kite flying are only a few of this site's helpful informational components.

Kites, Kids and Education
www.sound.net/~kiteguy/contents.htm

Given the title of *The Best Kite Site* by Kids, Kites and Education, this site includes a lot of interesting kite information your children will enjoy browsing through.

Kite Fantastic
www.kites.org/kitefantastic/

This site includes links to kite Web sites throughout Great Britain.

Kite Flier's Site
www.kfs.org/kites/

This site contains over 500 links to Web sites of interest to kite fliers and kite fans.

The Virtual Kite Zoo
www.kfs.org/kites/zoo/

Descriptions are given of many kinds of kites with links to kite plans and pictures that include historical information.

A Class Kite Day

Plan a special day for each child to make and fly his or her own kite. Try to choose a day when the weather will be cooperative. You will need to have access to a large, open field or an ample area where the children can spread out and fly their kites. The following is a sample plan for your kite day:

AM Morning Plan

- 9:00   Have the children watch a kite video (Resources, page 78).

- 9:30   Discuss kite decorating. Emphasize the importance of design simplicity, boldness, and color. Brainstorm some possible kite-skin designs.

- 9:45   Provide time to create drafts of their decorative kite skin designs on scrap paper.

- 10:15   Allow the children time to make and decorate Scott Sled kites using the step-by-step procedure (page 68). (**Note:** You will need several adults on hand to assist!)

- 11:30   Review the Kite-safety Rules (page 49) and Flying Tips (below).

- 11:45   Prepare to go outside by having the children gather up their (picnic-style) lunches and new kites and go to the kite site. (It is advisable that you have adult assistance in monitoring your children.)

PM Afternoon Plan

- 12:15   Everyone enjoys a picnic at the kite site.

- 12:40   Share a few historical facts: The Scott Sled Kite was invented by W. M. Allison, of Ohio, in 1950. He named the kite after Sir Walter Scott, the Scottish writer and kite innovator. It has two spines, which makes it look like a sled.

- 12:45   Demonstrate kite-flying methods, as well as safety procedures for your children. (You can do this yourself or invite a kite-flying expert.)

- 1:00   Allow children to fly their kites.

- 2:30   Return to your classroom. If there is enough time remaining in your school day, have the children share what they experienced at the kite site.

Flying Tips

1. Correct launching is important and may take a little practice. Explain the skills needed:
   - Make sure the wind is to your back.
   - Lay the kite on the ground, face up and facing you.
   - Let out about 8 feet (2.5 m) of flying line.
   - Step back, pulling the kite upward into a flying position so that the wind catches it.
   - Smoothly let out the flying line.

2. Once launched, keep the flying line taut and feed it out slowly or your kite will do a nosedive.

3. Monitor your flying line constantly for correct tension. Always keep your eyes open for fellow kite-fliers, people in the area, tree stumps, or stones.

4. If your flying line becomes tangled, it is easiest to cut out the tangled section and re-tie the line in the middle, leaving a small knot. Bring your kite down gently and make your needed repairs.

Scott Sled Kite

Materials

- one sheet of white, garbage-bag plastic, (39" x 35" or 1 m x 89 cm)
- scissors
- transparent tape
- two 1¼" (3 cm) sticky-tape squares
- two kite spines (35" or 89 cm long; ¼" or 6 mm round doweling) made of bamboo or any other light, yet strong material
- 5' (1.5 m) of string
- 100' (30 m) of string, securely attached to a 2" x 5" (5 cm x 13 cm) cardboard handle
- several colors of wide-tip, permanent, felt markers
- child-created kite designs (see AM Morning Plan, page 67)

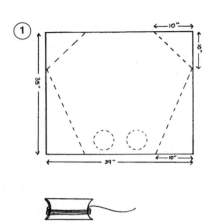

Directions

1. Using the dimensions illustrated above right, cut out the kite's skin from the garbage-bag plastic. Cut two 5" (13 cm) diameter holes near the bottom edge of the plastic.

2. Flip the kite skin over and place the spines on the plastic (as shown). Tape the spines in place using the transparent tape.

3. Attach the two sticky-tape squares to the outside "wing" corners for extra reinforcement. (This is where the bridle will be attached.)

4. Using the 5' (1.5 m) of string for the bridle, tape each end of the string to the reinforced corners using transparent tape. It is suggested that you leave approximately 1" (2.5 cm) of the string's ends protruding out so that they can be bent back and secured with transparent tape for extra strength. (*Optional:* For a stronger attachment, an adult can thread the bridle string on a needle and pull it through each reinforced corner, then knot and tape securely in place.)

5. Tie the handle string to the center of the attached bridle line to form a flying line by attaching it with a strong knot.

6. Use the felt markers to draw a design on the plastic skin.

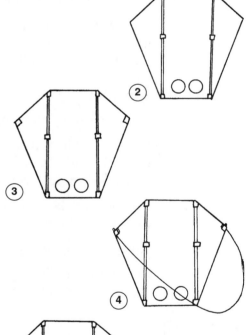

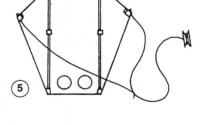

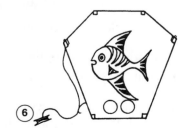

The Kite Stuff

Cover your chosen area with light-blue, bulletin-board paper. This will represent the background sky. Enlarge (if desired) and reproduce as many kite patterns (pages 70 and 71) as needed (one kite per child). Have the children color and cut out their kites. Then have them write their names on their kites; display. Your children's kite-related work can then be displayed near their kites, or you can use the bulletin board for whatever purpose suits your needs.

One idea is to write brainstormed children's responses on strips of colored paper when going through each stage of the KWL process and posting them on the bulletin board near that child's kite. A different color of paper can be used for each of the three stages (e.g. pink for want to know, etc.) making it easier to return to the board at a later time in the unit to revisit these concepts. This would work particularly well in a class where several children require personal recognition and reinforcement in order to "take ownership" of their learning.

Kite Patterns

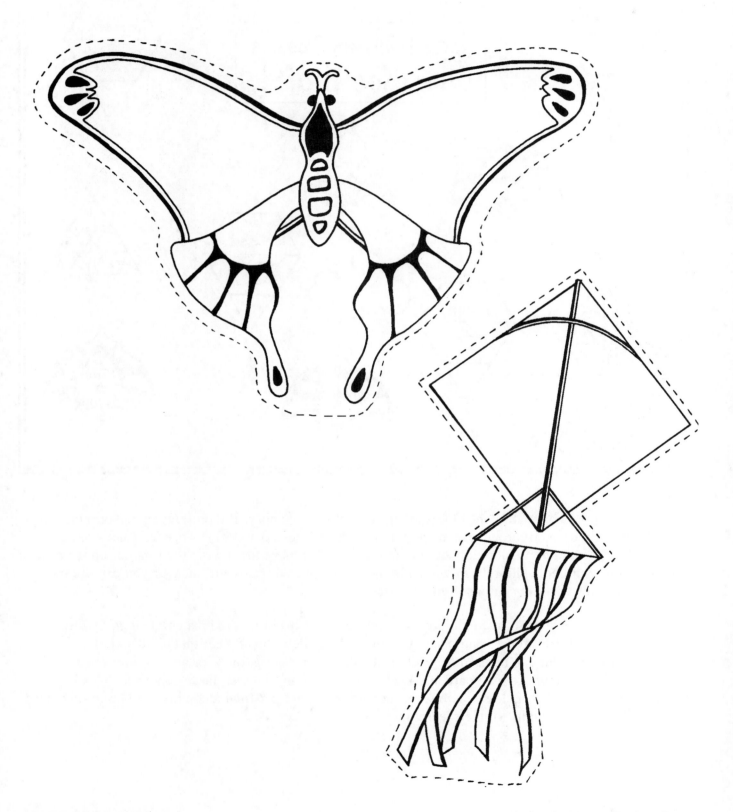

Kite Patterns *(cont.)*

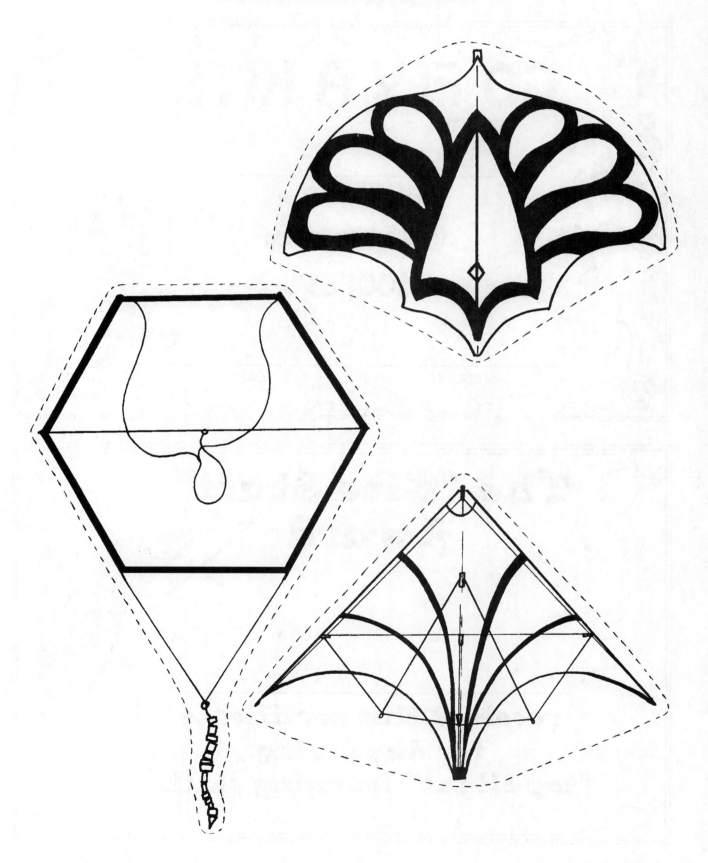

Kite Awards

GO FLY A KITE!

_____

(Child's Name)

flew a kite today.

Hooray!

_____   _____
Signature   Date

The "Kite Stuff" Award

_____

receives this certificate for displaying "top flight" learning skills!

Homework Task Cards

Use these task cards for homework assignments. Place the pre-cut task cards (you will need to make multiple copies of the same task card) in a jar and have each child draw out a card for his or her daily homework. (**Note:** The prepared cards can also be used for in-class extension assignments.) There is a blank card included so that you can create your own task cards as well.

Task Card 1

Make a poster of your favorite type of kite. Label the parts of the kite.

Task Card 2

Walk around your neighborhood and make a list of all the things you can see that could be hazardous (dangerous) for kite fliers.

Task Card 3

Look outside and observe the weather. Write two or three sentences about why/why not it is good/not good weather for flying a kite today.

Task Card 4

Design and make a kite bookmark. The bookmark may be shaped like a kite or you may draw kites on a rectangular piece of bookmark-size paper.

Task Card 5

Cut a medium-to-large kite shape out of colored paper. Find kite words or phrases in magazines (wind, amazing, blue and red, etc.). Cut out and glue the words to your paper kite.

Task Card 6

Pretend you are a kite. Draw a picture of what you see while flying high in the sky. Then write sentences or a paragraph about your picture.

Task Card 7

Make a kite mobile. Draw, color, and cut out four or five different kinds of kites. Hang them from a coat hanger using some string or yarn.

Task Card ____

_____

_____

_____

_____

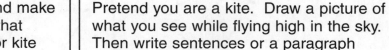

Kite Diagram

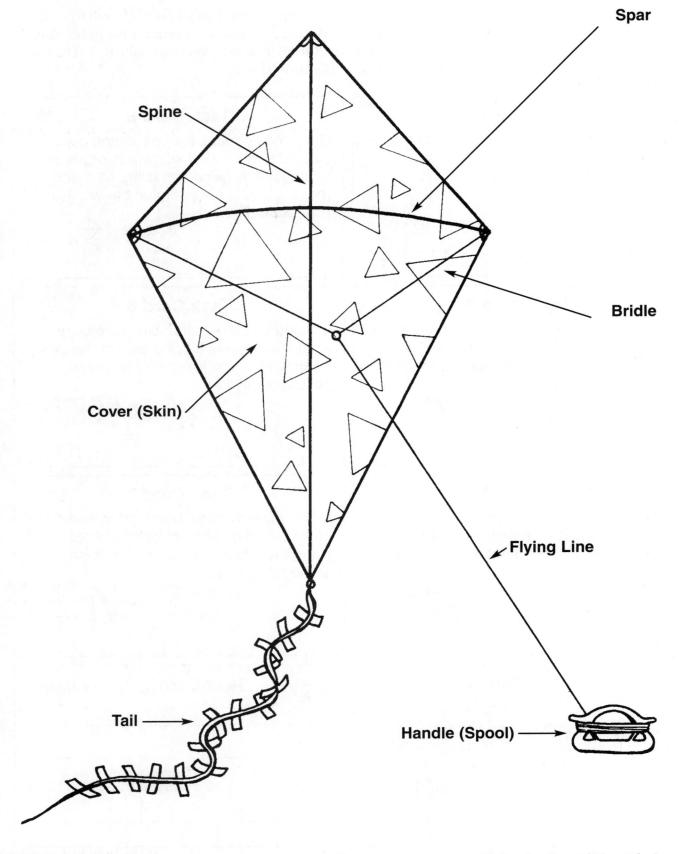

Spar

Spine

Bridle

Cover (Skin)

Flying Line

Tail

Handle (Spool)

Kites Glossary

Bowed kite

a kite with a curved spar and spine; therefore, it doesn't need a tail to fly

Box kite

a kite with open sections that allow air to pass through; thus, it flies well in strong winds

bridle

the bridle line for a kite is similar to a bridle for a horse. The bridle is attached to multiple places on a kite's frame to help spread the tension of the flying line across the surface of the kite

circle

a movement that makes a kite fly in a complete circle

cover

the fabric (silk, paper, plastic, nylon) that covers the kite frame

Delta kite

a triangle-shaped kite with a keel

dive

a movement that sends a flying kite straight down toward the ground

Fighter kite

a light, fast kite with a specially prepared flying line designed to cut the flying line of other Fighter kites

figure eight

a movement that makes a kite fly a pattern in the shape of the number eight

Flat kite

a simple, two-dimensional kite with a flat frame. Flat kites must have a tail to fly

flying line

cotton, nylon, or other synthetic fiber lines that are attached to a kite. The flying line is attached to the bridle, not the kite itself (except for Delta kites where it is attached to the keel)

handle

used for holding the extra flying line and maneuvering the kite

keel

a triangle-shaped piece of fabric attached to the middle of a Delta kite designed to spread the "pull" from the flying line and steady the kite in the air

land

to set a kite safely down onto the ground

launch

to get the kite up into the air

Parafoil kite

a type of Soft kite that looks like a parachute

skin

the fabric (silk, paper, plastic, nylon) which covers the kite frame, also known as a kite's cover

Sled kite

a kite which usually has only spines and a cover (no tail is needed); flies well in a light wind

Soft kite

a fabric kite which has no solid frame (no spars, no spines)

spars

fiberglass or wooden dowels that go across a kite (straight or diagonally)

spin

a movement that makes a kite turn in small, tight circles

spine

vertically-placed fiberglass or wooden dowels that run the entire length of the body of a kite

spool

a large, circular handle used for winding up the flying line and helping to control maneuvers

Stunt kite

a kite that usually has two or four flying lines that can be pulled gently to make the kite turn, circle, and spin

tail

a long piece of fabric, paper, or plastic which adds weight to the bottom of Flat kites so that they can fly (tails are sometimes added to other types of kites as decoration)

turn

a movement that makes a kite go in a new direction (e.g., move to the right or to the left)

Annotated Bibliography

Fiction

Ayres, Becky. *Victoria Flies High.* E.P. Dutton, 1990.
> With the help of a little magic, Victoria the pig is turned into a kite that has a chance of winning the big kite-flying contest. Grade 2 reading level picture book.

Berenstain, Stan & Berenstain, Jan. *The Berenstain Bears and the Big Red Kite.* Reader's Digest Kids, 1992.
> The bears make a big, plain, strong, red kite. At the kite-flying contest all the fancy kites scoff at Big Red, but none are strong enough to withstand the wind that springs up. Big Red stays aloft and wins the contest. Grades 1–2 reading level picture book.

Buckley, Helen E. *Moonlight Kite.* Lothrop, Lee & Shepard, 1997.
> The last three monks at a monastery have their lives enriched by the presence of children flying kites outside their walls. Grade 2 reading level picture book.

Ets, Marie H. *Gilberto and the Wind.* Puffin, 1963.
> Gilberto loves to play in the wind, but the wind sometimes frustrates him by taking his balloon, breaking his umbrella, or not allowing him to fly his kite. A Caldecott Honor Book. Grades 1–2 reading level picture book.

Lies, Brian. *Hamlet and the Enormous Chinese Dragon Kite.* Houghton Mifflin Co., 1994.
> Hamlet the pig tries flying a giant red dragon kite and ends up on an adventure. Grades 1–2 reading level picture book.

Ling, Bettina. *Kites.* Scholastic, 1994.
> Simple primer pattern book that is good for beginning readers. Its colorful kite illustrations are an added plus.

Luenn, Nancy. *The Dragon Kite.* Harcourt, Brace, Jovanovich, 1982.
> A crafty thief constructs a magnificent kite that he hopes will enable him to reach the golden dolphins that adorn the roof of a nearby castle. Grade 3 reading level picture book.

Nilsen, Anna. *Follow the Kite.* Picture Lions, 1997.
> Summary A simple kite book that includes a little, Flat kite attached to the book by a ribbon.

Reddix, Valerie. *Dragon Kite of the Autumn Moon.* Lothrop, Lee & Shepard, 1991.
> When his grandfather is sick, Tad-Tin goes out to fly his special Dragon kite so that it can fly all the family troubles away. Grades 2–3 reading level picture book.

Reeser, Michael. *Huan Ching and the Golden Fish.* Raintree/Steck-Vaughn, 1988.
> On Chung Yang Chieh, the kite-flying holiday in China, a grandfather and grandson compete in a kite-flying contest. Grades 1–2 reading level.

Rey, Margret. *Curious George Flies a Kite.* Houghton Mifflin, 1958.
> George is up to his usual mischief. He goes exploring, lets a bunny escape, tries to fish, helps Bill with his kite, and ends up having a strong wind carry him away! The man in the yellow hat comes to his rescue. Grades 1–2 reading level picture book.

Annotated Bibliography (cont.)

Fiction (cont.)

Roche, Hannah. *Corey's Kite.* De Agostini Editions Ltd, 1996.
Corey and his friends go to the park and fly their kites. Primer to Grade 1 reading level picture book.

Tibo, Gilles. *Simon and the Wind.* Tundra, 1989.
Simon, whose dreams know no limits, wants to fly with the wind. Failure does not disappoint him too much as he discovers that there are some things he can make fly. Grade 1 reading level picture book.

Trottier, Maxine. *The Tiny Kite of Eddie Wing.* Kane/Miller, 1996.
Eddie is too poor to buy a kite. An old man dreams of writing poetry, but can't. Together they are able to reach their dreams. Grades 1–2 reading level picture book.

Vaughan, Marcia K. *The Sea-Breeze Hotel.* Willa Perlman, 1992.
A fierce offshore wind discourages the guests from the Sea-Breeze Hotel until a boy makes kite-flying the major attraction. Grades 2–3 reading level picture book.

Nonfiction

Demi. *Kites: Magic Wishes That Fly Up to the Sky.* Crown, 1999.
This book starts with the legend of how holy painters first started painting peoples' wishes on kites so that the gods would grant their desires. The book also provides information about the different kinds of kite symbols and their meanings in China. Reading level is ages 4–8.

Dixon, Norma. *Kites.* Kids Can Press, 1995.
Provides background information on parts of a kite, materials/general instructions, kite decorating, how to make nine different types of kites, launching your kite, and kite safety rules.

Evans, David. *Fishing for Angels: The Magic of Kites.* Annick Press, 1991.
This book includes the origin of kites, kite stories and legends, a glossary, how to build a basic kite, and steps on how to fly a kite. Suitable for readers ages 10 and up.

Michael, David. *Step-by-Step Making Kites.* Kingfisher, 1993.
Provides an introduction to kite construction as well as directions for making various kites, such as a Two-stick kite, Box kite, Superstunter, and Windsock.

Morgan, Paul & Morgan, Helene. *The Book of Kites: The Complete Guide to Choosing, Making and Flying Kites.* Dorling Kindersley, 1992.
An excellent information source with full-color photographs on types of kites, kite history, and how to launch, fly, and make several different types of kites. The photographs help make the content information clear for non-readers.

Kite Resources

Kite Clubs and Organizations

American Kitefliers Association (AKA)

The AKA is a nonprofit organization dedicated to educating the public in the art, history, technology, and practice of building and flying kites. There are many kite clubs throughout North America connected to the AKA. To find one in your area, contact them directly or via their Web site: *www.aka.kite.org.*

352 Hungerford Drive
Rockville, MD 20850-4117

The Kite Society of Great Britain (KSGB)

The KSGB was founded in 1979 and has grown to be the leading organization for kite fliers in Great Britain, with over 3500 members worldwide.

P.O. Box 2274, Gt Horkesley
Colchester, Essex
England CO6 4AY

The Australia Kitefliers Association (AKA)

The AKA is Australia's largest kite society and was formed to foster and encourage the timeless art of kite-flying. Write them or visit them on-line: *www.moreinfo.com.au/aks/*

P.O. Box 738
Marsfield,
Australia NSW 2122

The British Columbia Kiteflier's Association (BCKA)

The BCKA was founded in 1980. It is open to all ages and levels of kite-flying expertise. Members frequently get together for Fun-Flys, workshops, and to participate in Kite Festivals throughout the world. Their Web site is: *www.bcka.bc.ca/bcka.htm.*

Magazines

Kite Lines

A quarterly journal of the Worldwide Kite Community. There is a world-wide kite calendar in each issue.

P.O. Box 66
Randallstown, MD 21133-0466

Kite Life

An online-kiting magazine.
www.kitelife.com/

American Kite

P.O. Box 699
Cedar Ridge, CA 95924-9984

Videos

Kite Crazy

A video designed to teach you how to build and fly kites. Meet kite flyers from all over the world. This video has excellent flying footage, is educational, and fun to watch! 102 minutes.

The Way to Fly

Provides "private lessons" with expert kite fliers. A great beginning-fliers training video. 32 minutes.

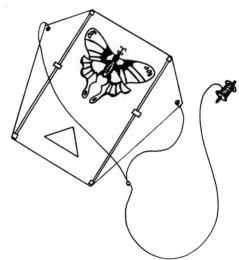

Answer Key

Page 14
bridle *C*
cover (skin) *B*
flying line *E*
handle (spool) *G*
spar *D*
spine *A*
tail *F*

Page 15
cover (skin) *D*
flying line *E*
handle (spool) *F*
keel *C*
spars *B*
spine *A*

Page 16
bridle *C*
cover (skin) *A*
flying line *D*
handle (spool) *E*
spines *B*

Page 17
bridle *C*
cover (skin) *D*
flying line *E*
handles (spools) *F*
spars *B*
spine *A*

Page 18

Page 19

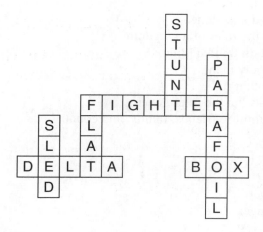

Page 28
1. Her name means "the smallest one."
2. He forgets her because she is so tiny.
3. Her favorite toy is a kite.
4. The evil men put the emperor in a tower.
5. She kept her father alive by flying a basket of food to his window with her kite.
6. Djeow Seow made a long rope. She flew it up to the window using her kite. The emperor then slid down the rope to safety.
7. Djeow Seow was the most loyal because she stayed near her father, and eventually, rescued him.

Page 29
Beginning
1. sad
2. happy
Middle
3. scared/worried
4. scared/worried
5. scared/sad
End
6. happy
7. scared/worried
8. happy

Page 30
1. smallest
2. alone
3. evil
4. tower
5. kite
6. food
7. monk
8. long
9. slid
10. prison
11. ruled
12. loved

Answer Key *(cont.)*

Page 31

tiny—small, little

lonely—sad and alone

emperor—the ruler of a kingdom

tower—a tall, thin building

monk—a holy man

robes—clothing

kingdom—what the ruler governs

loyal—faithful to friends, family, and country

Page 32

1. tiniest
2. older
3. bigger
4. stronger
5. loneliest
6. kindest
7. thicker
8. longer
9. bravest
10. most

Page 33

Djeow Seow:

- young
- child
- tiny
- ate alone
- played alone
- no one noticed her except the monk

The Emperor:

- old
- adult
- big
- daughters brought his food
- sons helped him
- busy man
- all his children served him

How they were the same:

- loyal
- brave
- rulers

Page 37

- try: fly, sky, my, I, high
- grow: blow, know, so
- deck: speck
- dime: time
- bite: kite
- cup: up
- bike: like

1. blow, know
2. fly, sky my
3. kite, like, time
4. April

Page 46

Page 55

Delta Kite

4 triangles

Sled Kite

2 circles

2 triangles

1 square

Korean Fighter Kite

1 circle

1 rectangle

2 triangles

Flat Kite

1 diamond

2 triangles

Page 56

Addition

See the kites soar high!

Subtraction

Kites are fun!